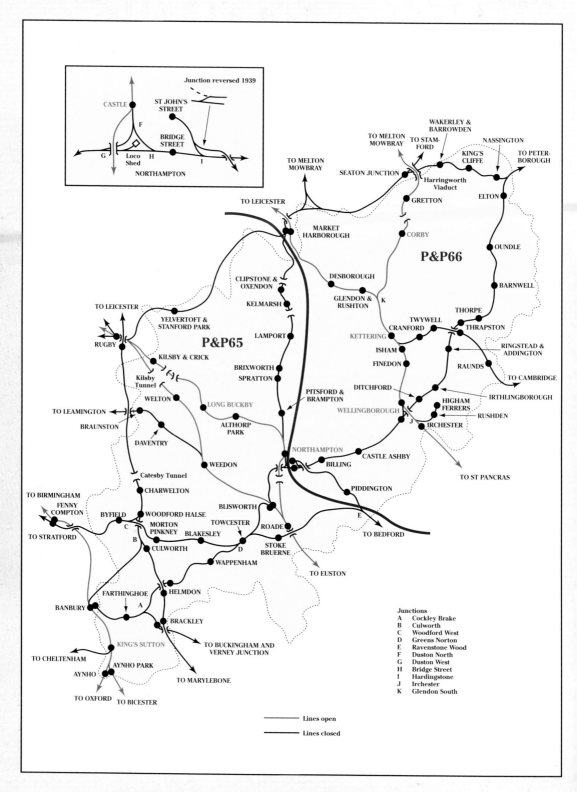

Map of the railways of Northamptonshire covered by Volumes 65 and 66, showing locations featured or referred to in the text.

BRITISH RAILWAYS

PAST and PRESENT

No 66

Northamptonshire
Part 2 North and East

Will Adams

Past and Present

Past & Present Publishing Ltd

In memory of
Ken Fairey
30 December 1924 - 15 December 2012
Lifelong railway enthusiast and photographer

Past & Present Publishing Ltd
The Trundle
Ringstead Road
Great Addington
Kettering
Northants NN14 4BW

First published in 2013

British Library Cataloguing in Pu

A catalogue record for this book
British Library.

ISBN 978 1 85895 285 7

ection.com
ollection.com

Czech Republic

ACKNOWLEDGEMENTS

As with Part 1 (Volume 65), my principal thanks must go to Northamptonshire railway enthusiasts and historians Peter Butler and Robin Cullup, who got this project off to a flying start by allowing me access to their extensive collections of photographs of the county's railways. These including not only their own pictures but also many from other photographers, in particular the ubiquitous and indispensable Henry Casserley and his son Richard. Michael Mensing and John Spencer Gilks once more proved invaluable sources of pictures, and were generous with their time in providing information. Thanks also to the late Ken Fairey, Gary Thornton, Tommy Tomalin and *all* the 'past' photographers credited individually herein, without whom this fascinating 'time travel' exercise would have been impossible. The source of some photographs has been lost over the years, so my sincere apologies if any have been wrongly attributed.

Thanks also to Bob Jarvis of Whitworth Bros, who kindly escorted me to the roof of the company's premises to take the picture on page 19, and to Frances Peacock of the Friends of Glendon & Rushton Station, for photographs and information.

Finally, once again Peter Butler and Robin Cullup cast their expert eyes over the text, but I must take responsibility for any remaining errors.

Will Adams
Denford
Northamptonshire

CONTENTS

BIBLIOGRAPHY

A good many books were consulted during research, but the principal ones were:

Bushell, George *LMS Locoman: Wellingborough footplate memories* (Bradford Barton, nd)
Butler, P. E. B. *The Rushden-Higham Ferrers Branch* (Author, 1994)
Butler, Peter *A History of the Railways of Northamptonshire* (Silver Link Publishing 2006; ISBN 978 1 85794 281 1)
Butlin, Ashley and Webster, Neil *Locomotive Lexicon* (Metro Enterprises, 1993)
Butt, R. V. J. *The Directory of Railway Stations* (Patrick Stephens Limited, 1995)
Clinker, C. R. *Clinker's Register of Closed Passenger Stations and Goods Depots* (Avon-Anglia, 1988)
Foster, R. D. & Instone, M. R. L. *Track Diagrams of the London & North Western Railway and its Successors, Section 5 Northamptonshire* (Wild Swan, 1988)
Marlow, Norman *Footplate and Signal Cabin* (George Allen & Unwin, 1956)
Midland Railway System Maps (The Distance Diagrams), Volume 3 (Peter Kay, no date)
Palmer, John *The Midland Line to London* (Grayson Publications, 1976)
Mitchell, Vic; Smith, Keith; Awdry, Christopher; and Mott, Allan *Branch Lines Around Huntingdon: Kettering to Cambridge* (Middleton Press, 1991)
Rhodes, John *The Kettering-Huntingdon Line* (The Oakwood Press, 1984)
Signalling Record Society (John Swift collection) *British Railways Layout Plans of the 1950s Vol 7* (Signalling Record Society 1994)
Tonks, Eric *The Ironstone Quarries of the Midlands, Part IV The Wellingborough Area* (Runpast Publishing, 1990)
Williams, Frederick S. *Williams's Midland Railway: Its Rise and Progress* (1876, 7th edition 1888, reprinted David & Charles, 1968)

The Internet has also been a valuable source of information, mostly I hope drawn from the more reliable of the many sites consulted! The Rail UK site (www.railuk.co.uk) was especially helpful for locomotive details.

HARRINGWORTH (or WELLAND) VIADUCT is one of Northamptonshire's best-known railway landmarks, although the northern end is in Rutland. It formed part of the Midland Railway's ambitious and expensive line from Manton Junction to Glendon South Junction north of Kettering, and is Britain's longest viaduct (except those in South London). Its 82 arches span 1,275 yards, and it crosses the broad Welland valley at a maximum height of 57 feet. Note that every ninth pier is a king pier with a pilaster. In the foreground of the undated 'past' view is Seaton Junction station, where the LNWR line from Market Harborough to Peterborough via Yarwell Junction left the original route via Stamford and the Midland Railway; it was also the junction for the Uppingham branch.

Although it carries a couple of regular passenger services, the line across the viaduct is principally used by freight traffic. The 'present' view shows how extensive repairs in blue brick have almost completely replaced the original relatively poor-quality red bricks used in its construction. Seaton Junction remains remarkably intact, but is now private property. *Robin Cullup collection/WA*

INTRODUCTION

As outlined in the Introduction to Part 1 (Volume 65), Northamptonshire's railway network has shrunk from a total of about 70 stations to just six, the three in this volume being Wellingborough, Kettering and Corby. Only two pre-Grouping railways' lines are featured herein – the Midland Railway (MR) and the London & North Western Railway (LNWR) – and it is only MR lines that survive today in the shape of the Midland main line and that through Corby to Manton Junction; all the more rural lines of both companies had closed by the end of the 1960s, except for some sections retained as goods sidings.

This means once again that the 'past and present' coverage presents a stark contrast between the surviving Midland main line, with its frequent service of fast and frequent diesel-electric units running between London St Pancras and Leicester, Nottingham and Derby (principally), as well as Corby since the reopening of its station, and the abandoned lines, now largely lost beneath at least 40 years worth of vegetation or redevelopment. However, there's plenty still to see if you seek it out; a long section of the Nene Valley line between Irthlingborough and Thrapston has been reopened as a footpath and cycleway, and a length of the Higham Ferrers branch is being gradually restored and reopened by the Rushden Historical Transport Society. You can also drive along some of the former railways: the A14 between Kettering and Thrapston largely follows the trackbed of the old MR branch to Huntingdon, while the course of the Nene Valley line between Barnwell and Oundle now forms the latter town's bypass.

The south-west of the county is arguably more picturesque than the north-east half, and the area covered in this volume has a greater industrial history, principally in the towns of Wellingborough and Kettering, yet even small towns such as Desborough, Raunds and Rushden have a rich industrial heritage. Ironstone quarrying and the associated smelting and the making of iron and steel have left an indelible mark on the landscape, not least in and around Corby, where the spectacular rise and fall of steel-making was closely associated with the railways, both the national network and many miles of mineral lines to the extensive outlying quarries. Iron-ore quarrying was developed from the 1850s into the 1870s, the LNWR's Peterborough branch providing an early impetus and eventually serving about half of the more than 30 quarries opened in the Wellingborough, Irthlingborough and Finedon areas. Only five were in production after the Second World War, although some lasted into the 1970s.

The first line visited in this volume is also one of the county's earliest, the London & Birmingham Railway (later LNWR) **Peterborough branch** – albeit a 'branch' some 47 miles long. It was built along the valley of the River Nene, with nearly all roads crossed on the level, which kept construction costs down and enabled it to be built in just over a year; however, it meant a total of 26 level crossings, a fact that counted against it when closure proposals were put forward. It was in fact Peterborough's first railway, opening in 1845, more than five years before the arrival of the Great Northern Railway, today's East Coast Main Line. Thus a Peterborough to London journey was initially rather indirect, via Blisworth to Euston. Built as a single line, it was quickly doubled by 1846. Once the GN line gave Peterborough a faster and more direct route to the capital, the Nene Valley branch became something of a byway, and remained so for the rest of its life. The last passenger trains ran on 2 May 1964, although the line remained open from Peterborough to Oundle for goods traffic and school specials until 1972, and its eastern end beyond Yarwell Junction is now operated by the thriving Nene Valley Railway heritage line.

The other LNWR line considered just sneaks into the north of the county at Welham Junction and Ashley & Weston, then between **Seaton Junction and Yarwell Junction**. Most of the LNWR's Rugby-Stamford line ran just outside the county border, offering services to Peterborough via the Midland Railway from Luffenham. To avoid having to use MR metals, the LNWR built a new line from Seaton to Yarwell Junction on the Nene Valley route, via higher ground that gave the route the enginemen's nickname of 'going over the Alps'. Three stations were in Northamptonshire: Wakerley & Barrowden, King's Cliffe and Nassington. Opened in 1879, the line closed completely in 1966 except as access to quarries at Nassington, which survived until 1970. There were also several hundred yards of another line in the county associated with the LNWR – the GN/LNW Joint line running north from Welham Junction towards Melton Mowbray and beyond.

The remaining railways were all Midland. That company's original access to London from its Derby heartland was in 1840, via Leicester and Rugby and thence to Euston. Then followed the Leicester & Hitchin Railway of 1857, built by the MR through Kettering, Wellingborough and Bedford to connect with the GNR at Hitchin, and thence to King's Cross. This line-sharing was impractical and inconvenient, so in 1863 the MR applied for its own line to the capital from Bedford, and what we now know as the **Midland main line** opened in 1868. In 1883 the line was quadrupled throughout to just north of Kettering, and from its provincial origins the MR had become a major Anglo-Scottish artery. However, despite today's good level of service between the East Midlands and London, sadly the route through the Pennines to Manchester, and to Scotland via the Settle & Carlisle line, are now but memories.

Four years after the MR main line opened, a **Northampton branch** was built from Oakley Junction, north of Bedford. There were three intermediate stations, each in a different county; the Northamptonshire one was Piddington. The terminus was at St John's Street in Northampton, replacing an earlier station used for Midland trains from Wellingborough, but when all the town's railways came under the LMS after 1923 it was clearly redundant, and closed on 3 July 1939, services being diverted over a realigned junction to Bridge Street and Castle. The branch closed in 1964, but an MoD depot at Piddington kept the Northampton end open, latterly in MoD ownership, until it was lifted in the 1980s.

Another branch from the MR main line, the **Higham Ferrers branch**, served Rushden and Higham Ferrers, towns with a strong boot-and-shoe-making industry that needed better railway connections. Somewhat reluctantly, it seems, the MR opened the branch in 1894, and it conveniently joined the new slow lines at Irchester Junction, following the quadrupling of 1883, without interfering with the fast lines. It also seems that the original plan was to continue north-east to join the Kettering-Huntingdon line at Raunds, but nothing came of this. The branch was a pre-Beeching casualty, losing its regular passenger service in June 1959. Occasional specials ran until 1968, and goods trains ceased in 1969. The station and goods shed at Rushden were bought by the local Council in 1976, and since 1984 the Rushden Historical Transport Society has slowly brought the station back to life, and laid new track towards Higham.

Between 1875 and 1879 the Midland Railway built a new line between **Kettering and Manton Junction** that bypassed Leicester, provided an alternative route for through traffic, and (like the Northampton Loop on the West Coast Main Line) effectively added a second pair of tracks (the main line from just north of Kettering being only double track to Leicester). It was a major undertaking, including Harringworth Viaduct and four tunnels in its 18 miles. Regular passenger services ceased in 1966, but Corby station has since reopened (twice), and the line is still a very useful (and scenic) diversionary route for freight and specials.

The final Northamptonshire line is another MR branch, from **Kettering to Huntingdon**. Beyond Huntingdon there was a short stretch of GN/GE Joint line to St Ives, then the Great Eastern Railway took trains on to Cambridge. Promoted and built by the Kettering, Thrapstone (sic) & Huntingdon Railway, that section opened in 1866 and was absorbed into the MR in 1897. It was always very much a rural cross-country branch with a sparse passenger service, but carried healthy iron-ore traffic at the western end. Consequently the line closed east of Kimbolton as early as 1959, but iron-ore traffic kept the Kettering-Twywell section occupied until the beginning of 1978.

We begin our journey by changing platforms at Blisworth for the Peterborough line to take a train down the Nene Valley...

Peterborough branch: Blisworth-Yarwell Junction

NORTHAMPTON BRIDGE STREET: The Peterborough branch swung northwards from the West Coast Main Line at Blisworth and followed an arm of the Grand Union Canal past Hunsbury Hill Ironworks before turning east to pass beneath the newer Northampton Castle-Roade line. Immediately there followed a triangular junction with what had originally been the Market Harborough branch (see Part 1). The north-to-west chord was controlled by Duston West Junction signal box, and here we are at Bridge Street Junction, with an unidentified Brush Type 2 (later Class 31) locomotive at the head of a train leaving the north-to-east chord of the triangle en route probably to Peterborough East. Behind the photographer on the left was Northampton loco shed, inside the triangle. In the right distance can be glimpsed Bridge Street station.

The line from Blisworth lost its passenger services in 1960 (closing completely in 1969) and that from Castle in 1964. Bridge Street Junction signal box closed in 1973 and much track rationalisation took place. The line through Bridge Street lingered on into the 1980s, serving some industrial premises and BR permanent way sidings at Brackmills and Bridge Street, as well as the MoD depot at Piddington. This elongated 'siding' seems to have been finally taken out of use in 2005. In 1986 a new Towcester Road bridge was built across the railway roughly where the junction signals are in the 'past' view, and it is from that bridge that the first 'present' picture was taken. As can be seen, a single track survives under the weeds, and one of Bridge Street's goods sheds can be seen on the right beyond the new houses.

The third view is looking the other way towards the site of Bridge Street Junction, with the surviving line curving north towards Castle station (see Part 1). *Butler Taylor collection/WA (2)*

NORTHAMPTON BRIDGE STREET station is seen here from the level crossing (the bridge in question being across the River Nene, between the station and the town). The station opened with the line in 1845; originally simply Northampton, it became Bridge Street in 1876. As can be seen on the right, the station buildings were in an attractive Jacobean style. We are looking west towards Bridge Street Junction on Sunday 9 August 1959 and a group of travellers appear to be off for a summer day out – to where, I wonder. Note the prize-winning gardens on the right.

The station closed in 1964 and sadly the buildings were demolished in 1969. The 'present' view is from the level crossing, looking into the site of the station. The roof of the surviving goods shed can just be glimpsed above the track at the far side of the crossing. The former down (eastbound) line still crosses the road, but there is little likelihood of traffic any time soon, despite the warning lights. The signal box, beside the up line behind the photographer, survived until 2006, when it was damaged by fire and demolished. *Les Hanson/WA*

NORTHAMPTON BRIDGE STREET:
A little further up Bridge Street towards the town stands this fine 'Goods and Grain Warehouse', formerly part of the Midland Railway's goods depot beside the LNWR line at Far Cotton. The first view is from the 1970s – only the decimalised price in the poster proves that it is not many decades earlier!

By 2000 the building is being renovated, and '15p in the £ off these gas fires' has given way to a poster behind the scaffolding for the Vengaboys' *A Party Album!*, a Top 10 smash in 1999/2000!

In 2012 the beautifully conserved property was being advertised as a 'Character Office Conversion'. *Peter Butler (2)/WA*

BILLING: Beyond Hardingstone Junction (see page 90), the first station east of Northampton was Billing. It opened as Billing Road in 1845, but lost the 'Road' in 1883. Being some distance from and on the opposite side of the Nene from the village of Billing, now absorbed by Northampton, the station was an early casualty, losing its passenger service on 6 October 1952. The first view, looking east, shows the station a year later, in 1953.

The second view, from the up platform, shows the same scene on 18 July 1958, still virtually intact – only the fire buckets on the right appear to have gone! Goods traffic continued to be handled until June 1964, then the signal box remained open for a further two years, closing with the line in August 1966.

Today the station house remains largely unchanged, with some extensions, and a new building has been added on the right roughly where the former waiting shelter had stood. The present owner of 'Billing Station House' allowed me to take the present-day picture in September 2012. *Peter Butler collection/H. C. Casserley/WA*

BILLING: BR Standard 2MT 2-6-2T No 84008 (new the year after the station closed) passes Billing level crossing and signal box on an unknown date with an eastbound local train. In the foreground can be seen one of the two goods sidings provided. The road bears no evidence of the crossing in the 2012 view. *Ian Lyman/WA*

Two years after closure, the signal box is seen here in course of demolition on 2 September 1968; it appears to have suffered a fire. Note the crossing gate wheel. *Michael Mensing*

CASTLE ASHBY station (named after the nearby seat of the Marquis of Northampton) opened as Castle Ashby (White Mill). It was renamed Castle Ashby & Earls Barton in 1869 (though fairly remote from both locations), and remained so until closure in 1964, despite only 'Castle Ashby' appearing on the nameboards visible in this 2 November 1963 picture of a Northampton-Peterborough train arriving behind 'Black Five' No 45044. Note the fine 1878 LNWR signal box, and the siding on the left with its separate crossing gates.

All trace of the station and level crossing has disappeared except for the 1858-built goods shed, which in 1984 was converted to become Dunkley's Restaurant. The shed's former canopy can be seen beyond the hedge, enclosed to incorporate two railway carriages built in 1924 and 1925, acquired and converted in the early 1980s, that form part of this very original railway-themed restaurant, complete with assorted railway artefacts and, ironically, a 'Beeching Room'. *John Spencer Gilks/WA*

HARDWATER CROSSING was yet another level crossing, where the Great Doddington-Wollaston road crossed the line. The small signal box opened in 1899 and closed when automatic half barriers replaced the hand-operated gates in July 1964. On 27 April of that year ex-LMS 2MT 2-6-2T No 41227 heads east with the local 'motor' from Northampton. The generally straight and level nature of the line is clearly seen.

The course of the railway here has survived by being used as access for the extraction of sand and gravel by Hanson. The notice at the gate behind the photographer still refers to the location as 'Hard Water Crossing'.
Ken Fairey/WA

WELLINGBOROUGH LONDON ROAD gained its suffix in 1924, when both of the town's stations came under the ownership of the LMS; the former MR station became 'Midland Road' at the same time. The main buildings were in an attractive 'Tudor' style. Again, the station stood adjacent to a level crossing on the A509 and what was then the A45; at that time the latter passed through the town before turning east towards Higham Ferrers and the East Coast ports. It is from the footbridge over the crossing that this picture was taken looking east on 30 April 1960. In the distance was a connection up to the Midland station; this was used by MR trains exercising the company's running powers over the LNWR to Northampton. After the station closed completely in 1966, the link from the MR was retained to serve the sidings around London Road and Irchester ironstone quarry, which sent out its last train of ore in 1969, before being finally taken out of use in 1982. On the left are the silos of Whitworth Brothers' Victoria Mills.

The station closed on 4 May 1964 and was demolished. During the 1970s the A45 was made into a dual carriageway and re-routed to bypass Wellingborough, crossing the A509 at the station site, which has been completely obliterated by the new road. This is the view today at the level of the elevated dual carriageway. The silos in the 'past' picture still stand behind the modern structures on the left. *R. M. Casserley/WA*

WELLINGBOROUGH LONDON ROAD: This is the view looking the other way from the footbridge, back towards Northampton. In late April 1961 ex-LMS 2MT 2-6-2T No 42104 runs into the station at the head of a Peterborough train composed of assorted carriages. The signpost shows that the A509 London Road headed south from Wellingborough, while the left turn was the A45. Note on the extreme left of the picture the base of the Little Irchester war memorial.

Approximately the same view is seen again in 2012. The new elevated A45 is just off the picture to the right, and the course of the railway is roughly through the gate towards the distant skip. What was the A45 is now a cul-de-sac leading only into Little Irchester village, and the war memorial has been sited on the opposite side of the A509, behind the camera. *Ken Fairey/WA*

WELLINGBOROUGH LONDON ROAD: The station is seen again in this wonderful aerial view taken from the top of one of Whitworth Brothers' buildings in about 1906, and full of delicious detail. On the right is the level crossing and Wellingborough Level Crossing signal box (1886-1969), together with the footbridge from which the earlier pictures were taken – note the dual steps, allowing passing pedestrians to cross when the gates were closed as well as giving access to both platforms. What was to become the A45 runs in front of the cottages, while the almost empty London Road (A509) heads away towards Wollaston and Olney. Note the absence of the war memorial at the junction opposite the pub – the horrors of the First World War are still some years away...

By kind permission of Whitworth Bros, I was allowed onto the roof of their silos to record the present-day view (albeit from a slightly different angle – the 1906 picture was probably taken from the roof of the lower brick building on the right of the photo). On the right can be seen the A45 flyover crossing London Road at the site of the level crossing. The pub and row of cottages have gone, replaced by more modern buildings, but the terraced houses of Little Irchester help to fix the view. The two white lorries are on London Road, now rather busier and more built-up than a century earlier. Note also the lakes in the right distance, the result of sand and gravel extraction along the course of the Nene and its attendant railway; they are a prominent feature all along the valley hereabouts. *Author's collection, via Roy Avis/WA*

DITCHFORD: Beyond the junction for the connection to the Midland station, and having passed beneath the MR line, the next stop was at Ditchford. In the meantime the railway had crossed the Nene, which is now south of the line, behind the photographer in this 11 May 1962 photograph of 'Black Five' No 45392 on an eastbound goods. The river here was a popular local destination for days out, but otherwise there is no adjacent habitation, and the station lost its passenger service on 1 November 1924. Goods were handled at the single siding until the early 1950s. Also nearby were several rail-connected ironstone quarries, giving rise to the 'Ditchford Treacle Mines' famed in local folklore! The crossing was controlled by an eight-lever ground frame on the platform, later moved next to the gates. Is that the photographer's car, with its door left open, suggesting a hasty exit to photograph the train?

The site of the level crossing can be seen in the slight levelling out of the road by the 'Keep Clear' sign and the photographer's car. The bridge over the Nene is long and narrow, and traffic lights control today's increased traffic flow. The station house is long gone. *H. C. Casserley/WA*

DITCHFORD: This trackside view, looking east, shows ex-LMS 5MT 2-6-0 No 42970 passing the crossing with an afternoon Peterborough-Northampton train on 30 April 1964, just a few days before closure of the line on 4 May.

As at Hardwater Crossing, the trackbed here has been used as access to an Anglian Water treatment works, ensuring that the course of the railway can be easily traced. *Ken Fairey/WA*

IRTHLINGBOROUGH: After passing more ironstone quarry connections, including an unusual ironstone *mine* at Irthlingborough that only ceased production in 1965, and crossing the Nene once more, the line reached Irthlingborough station. It had originally been called Higham Ferrers, reflecting the fact that it served that ancient market town, almost 50 years before it gained its own branch line courtesy of the Midland Railway (see page 95). In 1885 it became Higham Ferrers & Irthlingborough, to include its other neighbour on the other side the river, then Higham Ferrers was dropped altogether in 1910. This early LNWR-period postcard dates from some time after that, and shows the tall 25-lever 1887 signal box and (inevitably!) level crossing.

Many stations on this line were characterised by an ancient bridge over the Nene followed more or less immediately by a level crossing – in this case, the bridge dated from the 14th century and the road in question was the A6 from London to Carlisle. This double bottleneck became intolerable as road traffic increased, so in 1936 Leslie Hore-Belisha, the Minister of Transport (of 'beacon' fame), opened a new concrete viaduct across the valley, which can be seen in the background of the later, but undated, view. The LNWR signalling has been replaced by LMS examples.

The station closed with the withdrawal of passenger services in 1964, goods services went in 1966, the buildings were demolished in about 1970, and very little remains today. However, at this point some 4 miles of the trackbed has become a foot and cycle path all the way to Thrapston, by way of Stanwick Lakes, a country park managed by Rockingham Forest Trust. The well-surfaced path is seen here crossing the rather bleak site of the station, and the viaduct can be seen in the background. The goods yard and goods shed were over on the right. *Peter Butler collection/Douglas Thompson/WA*

Below The erstwhile A6 is seen in the first of these present-day views, and more than 40 years since the track was lifted fragments of rail are still in situ at the level crossing, together with the stop-block for the crossing gates between the tracks. The second view is looking west, with the viaduct just visible through the trees. *Both WA*

IRTHLINGBOROUGH station is seen again, this time from the up platform, and also looking west. The date is 1953, and the substantial and attractive station building is seen to advantage. Milepost 20 (from Blisworth) is mounted on the building on the down platform.

In the 'present' view the brick edging of the up platform can just be made out in the grass about a third of the way from the left-hand edge of the picture. *L&GRP/WA*

IRTHLINGBOROUGH: This fine panoramic view is from the 1936 A6 viaduct, looking east. The photograph is dated August 1967, and although the station is no longer served by passenger services, and goods trains ceased the previous year, the track remains in situ. Note the substantial goods shed behind the station building.

The tall tipping dock behind the signal box is still to be seen today, but not in this 2012 photograph looking along the thickly wooded track towards the former level crossing. *Peter Butler/WA*

This alternative view is from further north along the viaduct, and shows part of the ancient bridge and old road; the level crossing was at the right-hand edge of the picture. *WA*

RINGSTEAD & ADDINGTON: Convenient for an easy course along the valley, but less so for the two villages nominally served ('& Addington' was added in 1898), this was the next stop eastwards. Photographed from a departing westbound train on 29 April 1954, it can be seen that the platforms were staggered. On the left is the down platform, while the up platform is beyond the hut and level crossing, and the coal wagon being unloaded into a truck from one of the two public sidings. The open area on the right once held sidings for Butlin Bevan & Co's Ringstead ironstone quarries, which were in production between 1871 and 1891 and produced 1,000 tons a week at their peak.

The station closed entirely in the spring of 1964, and a farming acquaintance told me recently that he had bought the down platform and building for £5, to reuse the materials, especially the timber, on his farm. Today the Stanwick Lakes footpath passes through the site, and the crossing (providing access to a riverside marina) is still gated, to prevent cars using the footpath. An 'up' cyclist passes along what is now National Cycle Network route 71. *H. C. Casserley/WA*

RINGSTEAD & ADDINGTON: Seen from the level crossing, beyond the fine LNWR 'Caution' cast-iron sign ex-LNER 5MT 'B1' 4-6-0 No 61348 calls at the ivy-clad up platform with the 1.24pm westbound train on 7 November 1958.

Thinking that all trace of this fairly rudimentary station would have disappeared after nearly half a century, I was astonished to find the remains of one of the crossing gates behind a tubular metal farm gate in the adjacent hedge. The metal straps are clear to see in the close-up, and a few replacement lengths of timber are all that would be needed to restore the gate to its original condition! *John Spencer Gilks/WA (2)*

WOODFORD MILL: This glorious photograph was taken from the road between Ringstead and Great Addington looking east across the valley of the Nene on 8 June 1963. As the oilseed rape breaks into flower, a BR Standard 73XXX 4-6-0 rattles along towards Peterborough. Ringstead & Addington station is on the extreme right of the picture, where a goods train appears to be heading towards Northampton.

Forty-nine years and one day later, on a hazy 9 June 2012, the rape is more advanced, and so is the tree growth along the railway and river. No need to worry about present-day climate change being affected by lack of trees and hedges here! *John Spencer Gilks/WA*

WOODFORD MILL: That train was about to cross the River Nene by a substantial iron girder bridge, which can be seen in this photograph looking towards Northampton from the Ringstead-Addington road just above Woodford Mill. As mentioned in the Introduction, the line was built close to the river and construction costs were kept down by having nearly all road crossings on the level; thus the bridge here is, as far as I can see, the first road bridge across the line since Northampton, about 20 miles away! Heading towards Northampton on a misty Saturday 26 October 1963 is Brush diesel No D5578 (later Class 31 No 31160, less than four years old here) at the head of the 3.50pm service from Peterborough East.

The view from the road bridge is now obscured by foliage, so this is the view of the river bridge, fully restored, from 'track' level, still accessible by foot, bike or horse if you want to make a journey along the line today. *Michael Mensing/WA*

WOODFORD MILL: Looking from the other side of the bridge, north-eastwards towards Peterborough, ex-GER 'D16' 4-4-0 No 62599 (I think) heads a Northampton train past Ringstead & Addington's Up Distant signal, which was located some 950 yards from the crossing there. On the left, where the platelayers' hut stands, was the location of Newbridge Siding, where there was a tramway to a quarry near Great Addington in the 1870s and '80s; the sidings and signal box had gone by the end of the century.

The small noticeboard on the track at the site of the footpath crossing seen in the 'past' view advertises the tearoom at Woodford Mill, a great place to stop and have a cream tea or meal during your walk along the line. The refurbished mill, complete with water wheel and riverside garden, contains (at the time of writing) a model of Ringstead & Addington station. *Peter Waylett/WA*

ISLIP IRON COMPANY'S SIDING: Just before milepost 25½ the Peterborough branch passed beneath the MR's Kettering-Huntingdon line as the latter crossed the valley and river towards Thrapston Midland Road station (see page 123). The Islip Furnaces, fed by the largest narrow-gauge system of any ironstone quarry, were served by the MR line, and also by a spur from the LNWR that ran up beside the MR embankment. Interchange sidings were laid out in 1886 at the foot of the route, as can be seen in this photograph taken from the Midland line looking towards Thrapston. The last load of ore from the quarries was carried down in October 1952.

This is view from the Midland Railway overbridge (which is still in situ), looking more or less along the course of the LNWR line. This is now accessible open land, and on the right is further evidence of sand and gravel extraction – flooded workings now turned to advantage as a nature reserve. The spire of Thrapston parish church can just be glimpsed at the extreme right of both photographs. *Transport Treasury/WA*

ISLIP IRON COMPANY'S SIDING: This ground-level photograph shows ex-LNER 'B1' 4-6-0 No 61236 passing the 1886 signal box that controlled access to the iron company's sidings. The 15-lever box closed on 22 November 1965, and several of its main-line signals were 'slotted' (jointly worked) with Thrapston Bridge Street signal box, so close together were they. *Ivor Watson*

An 1880s map of the sidings, showing the LNWR's boundary and the limits of maintenance responsibility of both the LNWR and the iron company. *Robin Cullup collection*

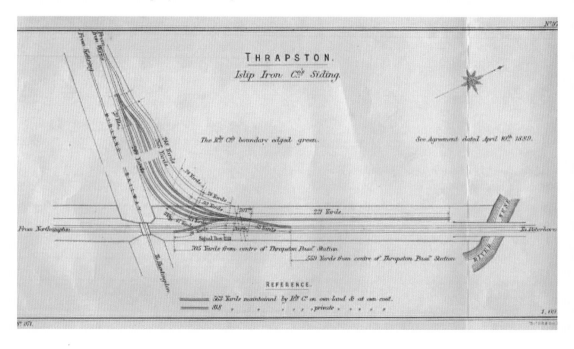

THRAPSTON BRIDGE STREET: Having crossed the Nene yet again, and with a sense of déjà vu, we enter Bridge Street station, as in Northampton, over a level crossing, the bridge in question being across the River Nene. This was the old A604 Kettering-Huntingdon road, and there was a 'triple whammy' here for westbound motorists: traffic lights in a narrow single-carriageway section of High Street, then the level crossing, then traffic lights on the ancient narrow river bridge. Demolition in the town, closure of the railway and the arrival of the A14 solved the problem. This view seems to have been taken from the rear of a departing Northampton-bound train on 29 April 1954; with smart work from the signalman, the signals are back at danger and he is at the wheel, the gates already starting to swing. As in Wellingborough, the distinguishing 'Bridge Street' suffix was added in 1924, when both of Thrapston's stations came under LMS ownership. The goods yard was at the far end of the station.

From the same viewpoint today there is no trace whatever of the station, the site now being a small industrial estate. However, behind the camera is an overgrown section of trackbed stretching back towards the piers of the river bridge, helping to fix the location of the level crossing. *H. C. Casserley/WA*

THORPE: This must be about level crossing No 15 since Northampton, at the modest wayside station serving the village of Thorpe Waterville. This is the A605 Higham Ferrers-Peterborough road. The 1880 signal box is on the extreme right of the considerably skewed level crossing, and the gates have been closed and signals lowered for a down train one damp day during the 1930s. A handful of wagons occupy the goods yard beyond the station.

The station building, much extended, and other railway houses (glimpsed along the road beyond the lorry in the 'past' view) are still in use as private residences. The track through the station is now a garden, but behind the camera the trackbed is more easily traced, with a small bridge across a stream immediately adjacent to the former crossing. *Lens of Sutton Association/WA*

BARNWELL: During the Casserleys' journey up the Peterborough branch on 29 April 1954 they also photographed Barnwell station as their train departed towards Northampton. On the left is the A605 again, with the level crossing on the side road to Barnwell village.

The station closed with all the others in May 1964, but the station house has survived as a private residence. This broader view of the remodelled road junction and former level crossing site shows that the building has recently been sensitively extended. The wooden waiting room beyond in the 'past' view was built in 1884 to accommodate Royal visitors to nearby Barnwell Manor, home of HRH the Duke of Gloucester (of No 71000 fame). In 1977 it was acquired by the Nene Valley Railway and moved by road to Wansford, where it now forms part of the heritage line's principal station. The car on the left is taking the route of the old A605 through the centre of Oundle, while the approaching lorry is on the Oundle bypass, which uses the Peterborough branch trackbed to the far end of the town. *R. M. Casserley/WA*

OUNDLE: The southerly approach to Oundle station was, you've guessed it, across a level crossing with, correct again, a bridge over the Nene just off the picture to the left. The station was photographed a few minutes before the previous picture. As can be seen, the platforms were staggered, with a foot crossing connecting their inner ends. Originally the goods facilities were on both sides of the line, connected by wagon turntables and a track crossing the running lines at right-angles between the platforms. Eventually the goods yard was concentrated on the up side. Although the Peterborough branch lost its regular passenger services in 1964, the Peterborough-Oundle section stayed open until 1972 for the benefit of pupils at Oundle School, and for goods until 1969.

More survives of the station than this 2012 equivalent view would indicate. The only link with the past in this photograph is the wall across the road from the signal box, which can be seen just to the left of the car passing on Station Road. *H. C. Casserley/WA*

After some years of dereliction, the station building has been restored to become a handsome private house. It was designed, like the other larger stations along the line, by prolific station designer John W. Livock, who was also responsible for Birmingham New Street, Atherstone, Buckingham, Wansford and many others. Railway architectural historian Gordon Biddle describes his work on this line as 'supreme examples of the early-19th-century picturesque movement applied to railways, with the utmost care paid to every detail.' Recently the goods yard has become a small housing development. *WA*

ELTON station opened in 1847, a couple of years after the line, and closed early, at the end of 1953; the station house was architecturally unlike its fellows. Although it had the obligatory level crossing, the signals were controlled from a lever frame on the station, which was reduced to ground frame status in 1956. At 4.10pm on 18 July 1959 ex-LMS 4F 0-6-0 No 44137 passes with a Northampton-bound passenger train.

We eventually found clues to the location: the slight dip in the road, the rising fence on the left, then – another 'Tony Robinson moment' – some rummaging in the blossoming hawthorn bush revealed a level crossing gate post, still complete with metal cap (centre of picture) – the far one on the left-hand side of the 'past' view.

Three-quarters of a mile further on the railway crossed the River Nene again and entered what is now Cambridgeshire (formerly the Soke of Peterborough), where it was joined by the line from Seaton Junction and headed towards Peterborough. *John Spencer Gilks/WA*

WAKERLEY & BARROWDEN station was just a few yards inside the county beside the River Welland, about 3¼ miles from Seaton Junction on the line 'over the Alps' to Yarwell Junction. Opened with the line on 1 November 1879, the station was on an embankment, with timber platforms and wooden station offices at first-floor level on a brick base. Climbing from the Welland valley with a lengthy down freight on Saturday 1 September 1962 is ex-LMS 5MT 2-6-0 No 42955. The signal box and goods yard were behind the camera at the east end of the station.

The station closed with the line in June 1966, and since the removal of the embankment the up-side station buildings on their brick base (on the left of the 'past' view) have been left 'high and dry'. An equivalent 'present' picture was not possible, so the buildings are seen here from the west end of the station; they have recently been much extended across the platform area. *John Spencer Gilks/WA*

FINESHADE: Cutting through the high ground between the valleys of the Welland and the Willow Brook, the line passed through Fineshade Wood. This photograph was taken on the same day as that opposite, and shows 'Black Five' 4-6-0 No 44836 at the head of the 1.50pm Saturdays-only Rugby-Peterborough East train, which left Seaton Junction at 2.42 and reached Peterborough at 3.09. The photograph was taken from the bridge carrying the lane to Fineshade Wood, now an extensive Forestry Commission area of mixed broadleaf and conifer woodland popular with walkers, horse-riders and cyclists, with a Visitor Centre and cafe. The cutting is thickly wooded today, so a 'present-day' picture would be meaningless. *John Spencer Gilks*

KING'S CLIFFE station served a sizeable village, and is seen in the first undated view during LMS days, looking west towards Seaton Junction. The platforms were of timber construction on concrete piers. On the left a lorry is tipping possibly ironstone or the buff-coloured limestone that was quarried nearby into a train of open wagons. There was never a footbridge here, passengers having to cross the line on the level, which led to three fatal accidents over the years. Originally the station buildings had three-ridged canopies over the platforms, corresponding to the three gables.

The second view is dated 27 August 1960 and is looking in the opposite direction towards Nassington. The down-side building is similar, but not identical, to that opposite, and is also missing its former canopy. Note that the LMS nameboard spells the location as one word without an apostrophe.

Tracing the station site was not too difficult, but finding any trace of the structures was very much a 'Time Team' operation. Eventually our metaphorical 'trowelling' amongst the undergrowth of what is now known as Willow Walk Pocket Park revealed among the saplings many of the piers that had once supported the platforms. The second 'present' view shows the car park for Willow Walk, and the right-hand edge appears to be the edge of the tipping platform seen in the LMS-era photograph. *Peter Butler collection/John Spencer Gilks/WA(2)*

NASSINGTON's down-side building was similar to that at King's Cliffe, although in timber, while the up platform had a ridge-roofed building and flat canopy. This is the view looking east towards Yarwell Junction in LMS days; beyond the bridge over Station Road are the LNWR signal box on the left and the goods shed and sidings on the right. This station's closure predated the others on the line, shutting its doors to passengers on 1 July 1957 and goods a month later. The signal box closed in 1965 and the goods yard connections were taken out of use. However, because of Nassington ironstone quarry a little to the west, opened in 1939, the line was retained. It was singled in 1966 when the up line was removed, and was not used regularly after 1971, although the Royal Train was stabled on it in that year, and as late as 1976 it was traversed by a Peterborough Railway Society special.

Today all trace of the station has gone, but the broader 'present' view shows that the station house is still occupied. The present owners kindly allowed me to take the equivalent photograph from the embankment (newly seeded with grass!). Beyond the now demolished bridge, the goods yard is occupied by industrial premises. A few yards beyond that, the line crossed the River Nene and entered Cambridgeshire at Yarwell Junction. *Douglas Thompson/WA*

Midland main line

IRCHESTER: The Midland Railway's main line entered Northamptonshire northbound as the passenger lines descended from Sharnbrook summit at 1 in 120. Less than a mile later was Irchester station, with platforms on the passenger lines only. It had opened with the Leicester & Hitchin line in 1857, and was renamed a little optimistically Irchester for Higham Ferrers in 1881, then Irchester for Rushden & Higham Ferrers in 1888. Once Rushden and Higham got their own branch in 1894, those places were dropped from Irchester's name. The goods lines were added in 1883 when the line was quadrupled as far north as Glendon North Junction. The station was unusual in that the station offices, in a 'half-timbered' style, were mounted on the road bridge across the tracks, as seen here on 13 April 1959. Note the photographer's car, 1934 Hillman Minx JY 4711, already encountered in Part 1.

The station closed on 7 March 1960, the station building was demolished, and a new parapet wall erected. The present photographer's car stands in for Mr Casserley senior's Hillman. *R. M. Casserley/WA*

IRCHESTER: Ex-LMS 8F 2-8-0 No 48332 climbs past the station on the goods lines, heading south on 20 May 1953. It can be seen that the goods lines are at a different level. The original line passed over Sharnbrook summit, about 3 miles up and 3 miles down at 1 in 119/120. This was too steep for the increasingly heavy coal trains heading for London, so the quadrupling from Irchester consisted of the 'Wymington deviation' of 1884, a second pair of tracks that swung east from the passenger lines at more gentle gradients of no more than 1 in 165 and passed through a tunnel beneath the summit – this saved a climb of as much as 40 feet.

The goods line was singled and brought up to passenger standard in 1987, perhaps a dubious economy as railway use continues to increase in the 21st century. Although the station is long gone, the station house and most of the goods yard buildings survive in private use. It has been suggested that the location might be ideal for a new local park-and-ride station, to be known as **Rushden Parkway**. *Peter Butler collection/WA*

IRCHESTER: This is the view north-west from the top of the steps leading down from the station building to the up platform on 13 April 1959. Irchester North signal box can be glimpsed in the distance. There was no connection between the two pairs of tracks here, but there was at Irchester South, at the beginning of the Wymington deviation. The North signal box closed a little after the station, in November 1964, and the goods yard followed a couple of months later. Irchester South box used to be the 'fringe' box for the West Hampstead, London, power signal box until 1987. All the surviving mechanical signal boxes north of there were taken out of use on 5 December of that year when the line came under the control of Leicester. Now West Hampstead works with the Kettering Workstation of the East Midlands Control Centre at Derby. The era of signalmen watching the progress of every train as it passed their boxes is long gone!

Included in the 'present' view are the supports for the former station building. The retaining wall behind the down platform can also still be seen. *H. C. Casserley/WA*

WELLINGBOROUGH MIDLAND ROAD: The line drops into the valley of the River Nene, crosses it and the LNWR Blisworth-Peterborough line, then swings north into the valley of the Ise. Wellingborough station ('Midland Road' was added in 1924) opened in 1857, and the central island platform was altered in 1894 when Higham branch trains began to use the station; there was also a bay, Platform 3, for trains to and from Northampton via the LNWR line. This is the view south from the island platform in August 1983 – the disused bay is on the left. The down HST is passing the wartime replacement Wellingborough Junction signal box, which controlled the junction with the connection to London Road station.

The box closed a few months later on 13 November 1983. Today's view contains little of interest; the bay platform face has been fenced off, and beyond it is the single goods line. *Both WA*

WELLINGBOROUGH MIDLAND ROAD: From a similar viewpoint we are now looking into the station. The end of the down bay can be seen, and standing in the up goods line platform, Platform 5, in this undated view but most probably the last day of passenger services on the Higham branch, 13 June 1959, is the 'Higham Flyer' push-pull train from Higham Ferrers and Rushden. The loco is in the middle and there is a driver's compartment at each end, which avoided the necessity of the locomotive having to 'run round' its train at the end of each journey.

That outer platform is now disused, the track lifted and the footbridge connection removed – indeed, an entirely new footbridge with lifts, the towers faced in local stone, was erected in 2011 to improve access at the station. The MR buildings on the island platform, complete with valanced canopy, can still be enjoyed. *WA collection/WA*

WELLINGBOROUGH MIDLAND ROAD: We are now on the down main Platform 1 looking north as Class 45 No 45121 approaches on 26 January 1980 (*below*). The 'Peaks', as they were known from the names carried by the first ten, were introduced to the Midland main line from 1959 as steam was gradually ousted. No 45121 entered service in December 1960 as No D18, and was withdrawn at the end of 1987. On the right is Wellingborough Station signal box, which controlled the north end of the station and access to sidings on both sides of the line. There was also a connection from down goods to down main, signalled by the bracket signal just in front of the box. This typically Midland-design 48-lever wooden box was opened in 1893 and taken out of use on 5 December 1987.

The second view (*right*) is only three years later, 4 July 1983, but the new order is represented by a High Speed Train set, introduced to the Midland main line in the early 1980s. Note the illuminated warning sign beside the barrow crossing, which reads 'Train Coming'. This was the only way of getting between platforms without the use of stairs until the new lifts were introduced.

By 2012 the signal box has gone and there is no need for passengers to cross the tracks on the level – indeed, it is wisely prohibited! Staple rolling stock on the line today is the Class 222 diesel-electric unit. The first of 23 Class 222s were introduced to the route by Midland Mainline on 31 April 2004, branded 'Meridians' and replacing the Class 170 'Turbostars'. No 222 007, seen here, was named *City of Derby* on 17 May 2007, and the units are now operated by East Midlands Trains. In the background of all three views is Mill Road bridge. *Frank Hornby/Gary Thornton/WA*

WELLINGBOROUGH MIDLAND ROAD: On 2 September 1898 a serious accident occurred at Wellingborough station. The 6.45pm Manchester express from St Pancras was approaching the station, and was running late – had it been on time the accident would have been averted. A luggage trolley, left on the down platform while a gate was opened, ran away and tipped off the platform onto the track. Despite attempts by staff to remove it, it was too late, and as they jumped for their lives the express hit the trolley. It fouled the leading wheels, and the locomotive ploughed along the line until it was derailed on points at the north end of the station and crashed. The wooden coaches were terribly smashed, five passengers and the two enginemen died in the crash and subsequent fire, and 60 were seriously injured. This contemporary photograph shows the aftermath of the crash, with debris still littering the down side. The large building on the far side of the line was the enginemen's hostel, or 'barracks', attached to Wellingborough loco shed.

On 29 May 1982 an unidentified but named Class 45 'Peak' passes under Mill Road bridge with a London-bound service, in uniform 'Corporate' blue and grey livery. In the foreground is the reception road for the down sidings, which for some reason was once known as the 'Tipperary', as recalled by George Bushell, who worked here in the 1930s (*LMS Locoman*, published by Bradford Barton). The hostel is long gone.

In a scene that is greener but sparser in detail – only the three running lines now exist – Class 222 No 222 005 approaches the station 30 years later on 9 June 2012. *Peter Butler collection/Gary Thornton/WA*

WELLINGBOROUGH MIDLAND ROAD: This is the view looking south from Mill Road bridge. On 29 July 1961 BR Standard 2MT 2-6-2T No 84006 gets away from the station with a down 'motor'. All four platforms are still in use, and on the right is a fan of five carriage sidings. Among the assortment of buildings beside the up goods line on the left, a couple look like the upper storeys of MR wooden signal boxes.

Some four years later, in 1965, a grubby-looking 'Peak' leaves the station. What appears to be a short breakdown or permanent way train stands in Platform 4 on the down goods line, and a Class 24 diesel is coupled to a rake of carriages on the right. By now Platform 5 is disused, following the closure of the Higham branch, and the footbridge extension has been removed.

Some 20 years later, on 5 May 1986, Class 45 No 45101 (the former No D96), in BR 'Corporate' livery and with the indicator box plated over, heads north. Wellingborough Junction box, in the distance, is out of use and its

signals have been removed. There has been much rationalisation of the signalling, and the carriage sidings have been turned into the North Car Park. A much plainer, uncovered footbridge has replaced the enclosed MR original. The station buildings on Platform 1 were designed by C. H. Driver in red brick offset by white and blue brickwork, with elaborate bargeboards. The round-headed windows contain typical MR lozenge panes. In that year, 1986, a sensitive and award-winning restoration and refurbishment was carried out.

By 2012 vegetation encroaches on the remaining lines as Class 222 No 222 009 pulls away from the station stop. The imposing new footbridge and lift structure can be seen at the south end. In 1876 F. S. Williams wrote of Wellingborough: 'Instead of being a quiet station in the midst of a purely agricultural district, it has been made the first great mineral and goods station on the Midland line out of London.' Today an 'agricultural' ambience would appear to have returned! However, all this will change in the years to come when the land east of the station (on the left) is built up as the 'Stanton Cross' development of 3,000 new homes. It is intended that the station will be enlarged with a controversial modern new building on the up side and a six-storey car park. Access from the town will be via a new road crossing the railway in the middle of this view, obliterating the North Car Park, to replace which the larger South Car Park has been laid out. *Ken Fairey/Peter Butler collection/Peter Butler/WA*

WELLINGBOROUGH LOCO SHED: The reason for Wellingborough being 'the first great mineral and goods station on the Midland line' was that it was 65 miles north of London, a convenient day's work for a goods engine; 'accordingly large locomotive establishments have been erected' (Williams). It was also about halfway between the capital and the East Midlands coalfields. The depot was north of Mill Road bridge on the up (east) side of the line, and here we see No 2 shed; both Nos 1 and 2 shed were square, but housed central 55-foot turntables with 24 radiating stabling tracks, the longest being those reaching into each corner. George Bushell recalls that between the two sheds 'was a shed with two roads through it, the one nearest the main line having the wheel

drop pit in it.' This is presumably the shed seen here on the right. 'In front of the wheel drop was the entrance road to No 2 shed... Between here and the back of Wellingborough North signal box were three stabling roads.' On the nearest road in this view from 21 May 1956 (*opposite above*) are two 8F 2-8-0s, with many other assorted locos beyond. Passing on the up main is a 'Jubilee' 4-6-0.

Wellingborough North box closed in 1962, and in this 1965 picture (*left*) it can be seen that No 2 shed has also been demolished. There are two diesel interlopers; the further away of the two is No D157, parked behind BR Standard 9F 2-10-0 No 92101. There's an intriguing ancient grounded coach body adjacent to the goods lines!

The shed, classified 15A by BR, closed in 1965, but happily the No 1 shed building of 1872 has survived in private commercial hands, as seen above on 29 May 1982 as a Class 46 heads towards the station. Cutting into the hillside in the foreground provided the material to form the broad level plateau opposite on which the shed stood. No 2 shed has been replaced by modern industrial premises, but a large elevated water tank survives.

In June 2012 Class 222 unit No 222 012 passes the former No 1 shed and the forest of silver birches now occupying the remainder of the site. Palisade fencing, graffiti and the Burton Latimer wind farm on the horizon complete the modern view. *Ken Fairey/Peter Butler collection/Gary Thornton/WA*

WELLINGBOROUGH LOCO SHED: We are now at the east end of Mill Road bridge looking north, with the No 1 shed building on the right. On 7 August 1956 a 'Black Five' 4-6-0 heads purposefully southwards. The line on the right is the exit from the shed complex, controlled by Wellingborough North's No 8 signal. On the left were once the Midland Brick Company's sidings; Williams tells us: 'In the various cuttings north of Wellingborough the clay is very heavy, and the banks, after they were made, slipped repeatedly.' Dominating the skyline is Wellingborough Ironworks. Iron ore extraction began locally in the 1870s for resale, but in the 1880s blast furnaces were erected to smelt the ore on site. Many quarries in the Finedon and Ditchford areas were linked by miles of narrow-gauge railways, which descended to the Midland line near Finedon Road, and burrowed under it to reach the ironworks. Smelting declined through the 1950s and into the 1960s, when only one furnace was alight, due to a falling demand for pig-iron. The works officially closed in October 1962, demolition was complete by mid-1964, and the land was sold to Wellingborough UDC for development as an industrial estate.

The down sidings, some ten in all, can be seen in more detail in the second view, from 7 February 1987, as an up InterCity 125 HST set passes. In the distance is the bridge carrying the road to Finedon, from which the adjacent signal box takes its name. Note how the remaining goods lines and former shed connections have been rationalised and slewed.

All is foliage in 2012 apart from the three running lines as unit No 222 001 represents the modern equivalent of the HST. The 21st-century communications mast has taken the place of the ironworks' blast furnaces!
Tom Rounthwaite/Gary Thornton/WA

WELLINGBOROUGH LOCO SHED: Looking south, the first illustration is an engraving from Williams's *Midland Railway*, captioned 'Locomotive Establishment, Wellingborough'. The three roofs of No 1 shed can be seen to the left of the exaggerated hill carrying the locomen's hostel, then a slightly fanciful representation of Mill Road bridge on the right.

For the second view (*below*) we move to 1931. A 4F 0-6-0 makes smoky progress along the up goods line, a Midland Railway 2-4-0 appears to be standing on the up passenger, and a 'Jinty' 0-6-0T is shunting in the down

sidings. The nearest wagon is from Netherseal Colliery near Burton-upon-Trent (incidentally, Sir Nigel Gresley is buried in Netherseal cemetery).

Twenty-seven years later, on 11 May 1958, Hughes/Fowler 'Crab' 2-6-0 No 42872, new from Crewe Works in 1930, passes with a down milk train – note the two 12-wheel Sleeping Cars at the head of the formation. Note also that the signal on the left has the same post, but the MR lower-quadrant arms have been swapped for LMS upper-quadrants.

Almost 60 years later the footpath from which the 'past' photographs were taken has disappeared, so this is a zoom-lens shot from the Finedon Road bridge. The roofs of the surviving loco shed building can be seen over the forest of silver birches,

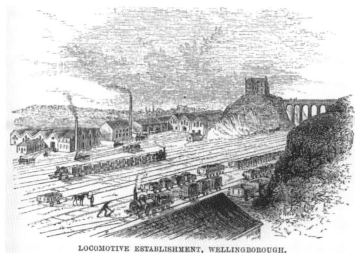

LOCOMOTIVE ESTABLISHMENT, WELLINGBOROUGH.

and standing in the down sidings is unit No C2102, a Loram rail-grinding train undertaking track maintenance for Network Rail. *Author's collection/Les Hanson/Ken Fairey/WA*

FINEDON ROAD: In this broader panorama looking south from the road bridge at Finedon Road, BR 9F 2-10-0 No 92084 heads a lengthy mixed freight along the down goods line on 25 March 1964. In the background is Wellingborough shed yard and the bulk of No 2 shed; the yard is full of rakes of empty mineral wagons, perhaps withdrawn? There used to be a crossover here between the up goods and the up passenger lines, and I wonder if it has recently been removed; there's a 'T' sign marking the end of a temporary speed restriction on the up passenger (beside the loco's tender), and lengths of rail and fragments of point 'frogs' lie in the 'six foot' in the foreground round the water crane.

The 9F is passing a gradient sign, which survives today, although all the other many familiar items of railway infrastructure have been swept away. The former up yard is behind the palisade fencing, although some the down sidings remain in use. The 9F was built in 1956, and withdrawn after a woefully short life in 1967, being scrapped the following year. *Alec Swain, Robin Cullup collection/WA*

FINEDON ROAD: Looking north from the same bridge on 25 May 1931, LMS 4P 'Compound' 4-4-0 No 1104 makes a superb sight as it heads south with an up express. Finedon Road signal box is just to the right of the loco's exhaust, while on the left are the sidings leading into the Wellingborough Iron Company's works. Just beyond these sidings, in the late 1880s, a line from the works to extensive quarries around Finedon, east of the line, burrowed beneath the Midland tracks. The connection between the up goods and up passenger lines referred to in the previous caption is just to the right of the loco. No 1104 (BR No 41104) was built in 1925 and withdrawn exactly 30 years later.

On 12 July 1980 staple motive power on the Midland main line is provided by the Class 45 diesel-electrics, the 'Peaks'. An unidentified member of the class is seen here. The ironworks has disappeared, replaced by an industrial estate, and the track layout has been rationalised. The splendid double telegraph poles have lost their multiple arms, and the signals, though all still semaphore, are now upper-quadrants. The small building above the second and third carriages is the South Sidings ground frame, controlling the south end of the extensive up reception lines and marshalling sidings. *Les Hanson/John Spencer Gilks*

FINEDON ROAD: On a sunny 3 February 1979 the open window of the signal box shows the 55-lever frame against the back wall. The up sidings are still busy, with wagonload and block train traffic. In the top left-hand corner can be seen a flat-roofed 1960s BR signal box at the north end of the yard. This is Neilson Sidings (not to be confused with the 1893 Neilsons Sidings box on the main line, just out of view to the left – the crucial 's' makes them clearly distinguishable…)

Finedon Road signal box closed on 5 December 1987, and has been demolished. The sidings were also lifted, but in recent years some have been relaid (as seen in the distance) as a depot for GB Railfreight, which, curiously, is a base for London Underground maintenance work as well as other freight services. On 12 July 2012 one of the ubiquitous Class 222 units heads north. *Peter Butler/WA*

NORTH OF FINEDON ROAD: It is Good Friday, 12 April 1963, and it's a period of transition on the Midland main line. Wellingborough ironworks can be seen on the right-hand horizon as former-Crosti-boilered BR 9F 2-10-0 No 92026 passes with a down iron-ore train. This type of boiler incorporated a feed-water heater beneath the normal boiler, through which exhaust gasses passed to pre-heat the water, before exhausting beside the cab. This ultimately disappointing innovation has been discontinued here, and the loco is exhausting conventionally.

What was then the modern era is represented a little later that evening by BR/Sulzer Type 4 No D146, at the head of the 6.10pm St Pancras-Nottingham Midland express. Ironically, the two locomotives were not dissimilar in age. The 9F was built in 1955 and the 'Peak' in 1961. However, the 9F had been scrapped by 1968, while D146, as Class 46 No 46009, left main-line work to enter departmental stock in 1983. It was then involved in a spectacular 90mph crash – a staged event at the Old Dalby test track in Leicestershire to test the survivability of nuclear flasks. On 17 July 1984 the loco and four Mark 1 coaches were driven at high speed into the flask on a rail wagon. Happily, the flask survived. Sadly, the erstwhile D146 didn't.

The greatest losses in 2012 at what is now known as 'Harrowden Junction' are the wonderful telegraph poles, and one of the goods lines, removed in the 1980s. *Michael Mensing (2)/WA*

FINEDON: By the time this picture of the station site was taken on 28 October 1973 it was long past its best. It opened with the Leicester-Hitchin line on 1 July 1857, but had closed as early as December 1940. The 30-lever signal box survived, as can be seen. It stood at what was once the north end of the up platform, which faced the main passenger lines only (on the left). Beyond the box there was a centre siding between the goods and passenger lines, that and the platform accounting for the distance between them. Goods traffic was handled until 1964, including traffic from the Excelsior stone works south of the station. In the right distance is a former Ministry of Supply depot. Note the positioning of the down goods line Home signal on the 'wrong' side of the line, to aid sighting beneath the road bridge. Today the view from the same bridge shows that only the 68¼ milepost on the right survives in its original position. *Peter Butler/WA*

FINEDON station building, on the down side of the passenger lines, was characteristic of others along the line with its elaborate bargeboards and round-headed windows with lozenge window panes. It is seen here on 2 October 1965, a quarter of a century after closure but still occupied. The up platform, between the tracks, has gone, and the down platform cut back.

Today's view from the road bridge has been broadened to include the parapet, to compensate somewhat for the fact that, sadly, the station building has since been demolished. *R. J. Essery, R. S. Carpenter collection/WA*

Opposite ISHAM station was only 1¼ miles north of Finedon, which may have influenced the latter's early closure. Isham fared slightly better than Finedon, not losing its passenger services until 1950. It was renamed Isham & Burton Latimer at an early date, as seen here, then in 1923 the LMS reversed the name to Burton Latimer for Isham. This early undated view, looking north, shows the neat and tidy station complete with flower beds on and off the platforms. The signal box can just be made out beyond the station on the down side, opposite the goods yard. The latter closed in 1964; the signal box ceased to signal the passenger lines in 1966, and closed the following year.

The wider 'present' view shows that happily the station building here still exists, in private hands, as does the old goods shed on the up side. The platforms have disappeared, together with the former up goods line. On the extreme right of the picture can be glimpsed the famous Weetabix factory. This was established here beside the railway in 1932 when the British & African Cereal Co was set up to produce a UK version of the Australian breakfast food Weet-Bix. The company acquired its present name in 1936, and remained a family-owned firm until 2004; a Chinese company is now the majority shareholder. The firm employs nearly 2,000 people on the 75-acre site, and all the wheat is sourced from farms within a 50-mile radius of Burton Latimer. *Lens of Sutton Association/WA*

PYTCHLEY JUNCTION: Between Isham and Kettering the MR's Huntingdon branch (see page 116) joined the main line, originally at Pytchley Junction. This rare undated but pre-1934 view, looking south, shows the signal box in the background, with the single-line branch joining the goods lines. MR Johnson 1P 2-4-0 No 266, hauling two coaches, has just come off the branch.

The signal box, which had opened in 1906, closed on 28 April 1935 and thereafter the Huntingdon branch joined the main line a little further north, at Kettering Junction. The railway here is on an embankment behind palisade fencing in a new housing estate, so a present-day equivalent shot was not possible. *Geoff Goslin collection via Peter Butler*

KETTERING JUNCTION: In this 5 July 1971 view, looking south towards the former Pytchley Junction, the Huntingdon branch, by now only serving ironstone quarries at Twywell, joins the goods line just beyond the signal box. The box was originally on the opposite side of the line, but was replaced by the one seen here in 1935 when the earlier box and Pytchley Junction closed. Norman Marlow, who worked the box in the 1940s (see the Bibliography), remembered that, though relatively modern, it was still oil-lit and there was no water supply. Note again those magnificent telegraph poles!

The box closed on 5 December 1987, and in the wooded cutting today it can be seen that the double-track slow lines through Kettering station are here reduced to one, and there is a 'ladder'-type junction across all the lines rather than the former double-track connection. *Peter Butler/WA*

KETTERING JUNCTION: Looking north from the other side of the Pytchley Road bridge on 27 March 1937, LMS Fowler 7F 0-8-0 No 9510 rumbles south on the up slow line. It is signalled to continue onto the up goods line; the slightly taller signal on the right is for the Huntingdon branch, and the tallest, on the left, is for the crossover to the up passenger line. It is interesting that the Huntingdon line signal is taller than that for the 'through' route – but at this point the up slow became the up goods, which would ordinarily not carry any passenger trains, so is presumably seen as the subsidiary route. The 7F, which entered traffic in 1929, was withdrawn in 1951.

There is not much to say about the 'present' view except to note that housing now covers what in 1937 was open farmland south of Kettering. *H. F. Wheeller, R. S. Carpenter collection/WA*

KETTERING SOUTH: Since Wellingborough the line has been steadily climbing, and here it leaves the valley of the River Ise and curves round the west of the town of Kettering. Less than a mile north of Kettering Junction was Kettering South, the junction conveniently crossed by a footbridge. Approaching on the down slow line on 18 July 1958, and signalled into the station, is 'Black Five' 4-6-0 No 44861 with the 5.20pm local. Note the elegant MR semaphore arms on the wooden-post junction signal, and the more modern upper-quadrant examples on the lattice-post signal opposite. The 'Black Five' lasted almost to the very end of steam, being withdrawn in April 1968.

The 'present' view is slightly deceptive, in that East Midlands Class 222 'Meridian' unit No 222 022 is actually running southbound on the down slow line, and will regain the main up line at the former Kettering Junction. Note again how housing has covered the former farmland. *Ken Fairey/WA*

KETTERING SOUTH: Moving to the east side of the bridge a year earlier, on 15 June 1957, we see one of the mighty Beyer-Garratt 2-6-0+0-6-2 locomotives, No 47982, built in 1930. In LMS days the Toton-Cricklewood coal trains represented a lucrative traffic, but were generally uneconomically double-headed. The Beyer-Garratt design provided the answer, being essentially two 2-6-0 locos manned by a single crew; as LMS President Sir Josiah Stamp remarked, '…in addition to saving one set of men per train, they will displace 68 old freight tender engines.' The production locos had steam-driven rotary coal bunkers, as seen here; the conical, inclined bunker could be revolved in about 30 seconds, moving the coal forward to the shovelling plate, thus removing a tiresome and time-consuming job for the fireman. No 47982, seen here with a long train of empties returning to Toton, is in the last months of its life; it was withdrawn on the last day of that year.

Performing heavy freight duties on the Midland on 14 June 2012 is an unidentified American-built Class 66 in Freightliner livery, heading south with a block train of tankers. *Stanley Creer, Robin Cullup collection/WA*

KETTERING SOUTH: Looking north from the same bridge, the 45-lever signal box can be seen on the left. In the first view, dated 30 October 1923, in the first year of the LMS, 4P Compound 4-4-0 No 1013 still has 'MR' on its buffer-beam as it heads south with an express. This loco, built by the Midland Railway in 1905, was withdrawn from Bedford shed in 1949. The gantry behind the train carries Kettering Junction's Distant arms, some 1,380 yards from the latter box – quite a pull for the signalman, especially as the line was on a curve, adding to the resistance on the wires!

Thirty-eight years later a former LMS locomotive, 'Jubilee' Class 4-6-0 No 45634 *Trinidad*, passes the same spot with an up express from Manchester Piccadilly on a misty 9 November 1961. The signal box has been spruced up a little, and carries a London Midland Region enamel nameboard. An up local train appears to be travelling along the up slow line. *Trinidad* had only two more years of service left, being withdrawn in 1963.

Kettering South signal box closed on 19 November 1967, and although invisible in the foliage the brick-built recess in which it stood still survives. The absence of the junction and a deal of track rationalisation are evident as Class 222 No 222 023 heads for St Pancras. *W. L. Good, Gordon Coltas Photographic Trust collection via Robin Cullup/Ken Fairey/WA*

KETTERING SOUTH: Seen from the centre of the footbridge on an unknown date, a mineral train hauled by tender-first ex-LMS 8F 2-8-0 No 48356 crosses from the slow to the fast lines. It has possibly come from Cranford on the Huntingdon branch, and is loaded with ironstone. The wagons look half empty, but that is because ironstone is much heavier than the coal for which they were designed. These 16-ton mineral wagons were converted to tipplers by the simple expedient of having their side doors welded shut. As can be seen, there were many sidings on both sides of the line, as well as centre sidings between the slow and fast lines, here storing what may be empty passenger stock.

According to official records the last train of ironstone left the Huntingdon branch in January 1978. The present-day view shows Bardon Aggregates-liveried Class 66 No 66023 with a northbound Lafarge block cement train. *Robin Cullup collection/WA*

KETTERING: This timely photograph, looking south from the up slow line platform on 25 April 1987, shows the signalling at Kettering in transition. Colour light signals have been installed but are not yet in use; the remaining semaphore signals would remain until Kettering Station signal box, seen in the right background, was abolished on 5 December of that year. Note that the centre sidings have been lifted, leaving the box rather isolated. On the left of the canopy supports (and the traditional platform barrows, a long-vanished sight) is the bay platform that used to accommodate trains to and from the Cambridge line. Reversing out of the station is a Class 108 DMU, which had arrived forming a service from Corby. Note that the new signal over the down slow is for the down direction only, facing away from the camera – bi-directional operation of the lines through the station, controlled from Leicester in 2012, was yet to come.

Happily, the 1913-built Kettering Station box was given Grade II listed status in 1981, and when it closed in 1987 it was acquired by Midland Railway-Butterley (the former Midland Railway Centre) and moved during the weekend of 4/5 June 1988 to that heritage line's Swanwick Junction, where it was recommissioned in 1990 and can thus still be enjoyed today. The rather utilitarian canopies at the south end of the station were replaced in 2000 with a smart new footbridge and lifts linking all platforms; formerly the only link was a rather dingy, low-roofed subway, which is now closed. The former up sidings have become the station's South Car Park. *Frank Hornby/WA*

KETTERING: Standing towards the north end of the down slow platform on 3 July 1937 is veteran Midland Railway '156' Class 2-4-0 No 20012, which has arrived with the 2.54pm train from Cambridge – nothing heavier than a 2-4-0 was allowed to cross the wooden bridges beyond Huntingdon. The station opened with the Leicester to Hitchin line on 8 May 1857 and was designed by C. H. Driver. It was enlarged in 1879 and altered again in 1884 when the line was quadrupled, and the station building was rebuilt in 1895. The 'ridge and furrow' glazed canopies help to make this one of best remaining examples of Midland architecture; in *Britain's Historic Railway Buildings* Gordon Biddle writes, 'Some of the most delicate cast ironwork anywhere graces Platforms 2 and 3 (an island) and No 4 at Kettering.'

By the 1970s maintenance of the canopies was becoming a problem, and British Rail proposed replacing the glass with plastic sheeting. Happily Kettering Civic Society objected and the canopies and columns were reprieved, and sympathetically restored by Railtrack in 2000. Only new platform surfacing, new lighting and the addition of a glass waiting shelter has changed the view in 2012. *H. C. Casserley/WA*

KETTERING: Here is another pre-war shot of the station, this time looking north. On 27 March 1937 LMS 8F 2-8-0 No 8003, at that time barely two years old, runs through the up slow line platform with a lengthy mineral train. On the right can be seen the coaling stage of Kettering loco shed, which lay adjacent to the station. In the distance is Kettering North signal box, which controlled access to the shed and a crossover between the slow and fast lines, corresponding to South box's fast-to-slow-lines crossover. Like South, North box closed in November 1967.

Today the platforms have new surfacing and modern lights. The former shed area over the right is now the station's North Car Park. Note the bi-directional signalling of all the running lines. *H. F. Wheeller, R. S. Carpenter collection/WA*

KETTERING LOCO SHED, opened in 1865, was a four-road straight shed, and the first view shows it on a sunny 3 September 1933, as a group of enthusiasts busily write down the loco numbers. This is the view of the east side of the shed yard, taken from the coaling stage. On the left is 2-4-0 No 12, the same loco that we saw earlier on page 76 bearing its LMS number 20012. In the centre is ex-MR 0-6-0 No 3157. Note the water tower on the extreme right of the photograph, the foundations of which are still to be seen in the station car park today.

Moving on 30 years there's a new generation of steam on the west side of the coaling stage, and a new generation of spotters! It is 31 May 1953 and on the left is the first Ivatt 2MT 2-6-0, No 46400, which was allocated new to Kettering in 1946 to work the Cambridge line. In the middle distance is sister loco No 46496, also allocated new for Cambridge trains. In the shed entrance is an 8F 2-8-0, then on the right is Kettering's ex-Midland Railway 4F 0-6-0 No 43898. Built in 1919 to a 1911 design, this veteran saw out its days at Bedford shed in 1957.

The third view is dated a year or so later, 7 August 1954, with yet another stage in loco development. On the left is almost brand-new No 78028, the BR Standard version of the Ivatt 2-6-0. Much older is the ex-GER 'J15' 0-6-0 in the centre; it is difficult to make out the number clearly, but it may be No 65390, one of the locos working out of Cambridge shed on the Kettering services. If so, this veteran was built in 1900, and was withdrawn in 1958 from Neasden shed. On the right is ex-LMS 3MT 2-6-2T No 40022; built in 1931, it was the last survivor of a class of 70 engines when it was withdrawn from Cricklewood shed in 1962.

As already mentioned, the shed yard is now the station's North Car Park, but the platform building on the extreme right is the same as that seen in the 1954 photograph, albeit a little cleaner today and minus its chimneys; in 1954 the four-pane window is all but invisible under the grime. *H. C. Casserley/Frank Hornby/Ken Fairey/WA*

KETTERING: In this busy panorama of the north end of the station in 1935, the loco shed can be seen again on the left. At Platform 2 is a northbound local behind 4-4-0 No 424. These engines represented the final development of Midland Railway 4-4-0s, from a design by Johnson but altered over the years by both Deeley and Fowler. No 424 was built in 1896 and lasted until 1951. The rear of an up service can be seen in Platform 3, while a 4-4-0 Compound is at the head of a down train in Platform 4.

By happy coincidence, at 17.29 on 14 June 2012 the same platforms were likewise occupied by trains, although less of a mouth-watering variety – all Class 222 'Meridian' units! In Platform 3 is the late-running southbound 17.15 service to St Pancras, while up and down services stand at Platforms 3 and 4. The clearly recognisable MR station of old is now framed by a large signal gantry, while the new footbridge and lift towers dominate the far end. *Lens of Sutton Association/WA*

KETTERING: Getting away northwards from Kettering on an unknown date, but seemingly a warm summer's day, is 'Black Five' 4-6-0 No 44661 with a down express. The location is looking north between the Northampton Road and Rothwell Road underbridges. In the distance the chimney indicates the presence of Kettering ironworks. These were served by railway sidings in MR days, controlled by the descriptively named Kettering Iron & Coal Co's Sidings signal box, which closed in 1967; nationalised in 1951, the site was acquired by Stewarts & Lloyds in 1956.

To illustrate the occasional woes experienced by the 'past and present' photographer, to reach the same location today I had to follow a muddy, malodorous and overgrown footpath from Rothwell Road into an area of thickly wooded wasteland adjacent to the line. Crashing through the nettles and brambles, I poked my camera through the palisade fencing to capture this rather unconvincing shot of the same location today. The former fields to the left of the line are now occupied by Kettering General Hospital, while the ironworks site has given way to the Telford Way Industrial Estate. Only an old path called Furnace Lane gives anything away. *Robin Cullup collection/WA*

GLENDON SOUTH JUNCTION: 'Leaving Kettering, we rise up a heavy incline,' wrote Williams in 1888. 'The new line to Manton runs parallel with us then bears away to the right...' Descending the 1 in 118 gradient on the up fast line towards Kettering in pre-Grouping days is an MR 2-4-0 with a local passenger train. In the distance is Glendon South Junction, where the Corby and Manton line curves away north-eastwards while the main line turns west towards the summit of the line near Desborough. There is evidence of ironstone quarrying on the horizon; the Glendon Ironstone Sidings were connected with the Corby line round the corner. Very often these deposits were discovered when the railways were being built, and provided valuable traffic for the completed lines.

North of Kettering the slow lines have been singled once again, as seen in the 'present' view as a Class 222 unit heads south through the now heavily wooded cutting. *Robin Cullup collection/WA*

GLENDON SOUTH JUNCTION signal box only controlled the slow lines and the junction with the Manton line. As can be seen, the slow lines were at a lower level here, and the box was tucked into the shallow cutting with its back hard against the fast lines. Apparently it was not unknown for lumps of coal from fast-moving up trains rushing down the gradient to come in through the box windows! On Sunday 4 April 1971 a Class 45 leaves the Manton line with a (presumably diverted) express from Nottingham. The line straight ahead from the junction joined the fast lines at Glendon North Junction, where the quadruple track finally ended after having been continuous for more than 75 miles from St Pancras.

Glendon South closed on 3 June 1973, and this sad picture taken a month later shows the remains in course of demolition, including the 16-lever frame. The signalling was taken over by Glendon North, 673 yards away, from then until the latter's closure in 1987, which meant that trains on the Corby line could only be seen by the signalman over the fields at the rear of the box! He could not see the tail lamps, so had to wait for 'Train out of section' from the next boxes north or south before being able to send that signal himself.

As already mentioned, the cutting is now heavily overgrown, but I managed to snatch this shot of the site of the signal box. There is no junction here now – the single slow line curves round towards Corby, and there is no longer a connection to Glendon North. *John Spencer Gilks/Peter Butler/WA*

GLENDON & RUSHTON was another station designed by C. H. Driver (who was also responsible for Desborough, the original Kettering building, and Finedon). Opened simply as Rushton, it took its later name in 1896, helping to distinguish it from the Midland's Rushden station, also in the county! The 'past' picture shows the station looking west in 1960, the year that passenger services ceased, although goods traffic continued for a further five years.

The station was awarded Grade II listed status in 1981, and in 1987 BR sold it and some housing development took place in the yard, resulting in the sad loss of the goods shed. In 2004 the property was sold again. The family of Mr

Beswick, the last station master, continued to occupy the building as statutory tenants, but it began to fall into a serious state of disrepair. The 'present' picture shows the station buildings in the state they are today. With the agreement of the present owner, who was denied planning permission to further develop the site, the Friends of Glendon & Rushton Station started looking after the station with the aim of restoring the building and hopefully eventually buying it, to ensure its survival for future generations to enjoy. For more details visit http://nicwhe8.freehostia.com/ glendonrushton/. *Photos courtesy of Friends of Glendon & Rushton Station*

DESBOROUGH had 'for Rothwell' added to its name within months of opening in 1857, and in 1899 the two towns became equal partners in Desborough & Rothwell. This is the east end of the station on a sunny autumn morning; at 9.25am on 17 October 1964 ex-LMS 8F 2-8-0 No 48644 heads southwards with a coal train, while the tail end of the 8.05am St Pancras-Manchester express can be seen disappearing towards the station. The coal train is passing the 19-lever Desborough Station signal box, which closed on 26 May 1968, not long after the station itself had closed on New Year's Day. The sidings on the right served quarries stretching a mile and a half north-east of the station, originally operated by the Chesterfield-based Sheepbridge Iron Co, later part of Stewarts & Lloyds. The quarries operated until the 1960s, and the last surviving steam loco in use was purchased for preservation.

Because of tree growth the 'present' picture is taken from the crown of the road bridge. The goods yard is now occupied by various firms, including a shed company, and there is no trace of any of the other features in the 'past' picture. Although the station has disappeared, the attractive Midland-style station house survives in private hands. *Tommy Tomalin/WA*

DESBOROUGH: The bridge from which the previous pictures were taken can be seen in the distance as Ivatt 4MT 2-6-0 No 43042 approaches the station with a local train for Leicester on 30 May 1959. This was the last LMS locomotive design to appear before nationalisation, and had a somewhat unprepossessing look, with a very high running plate above the cylinders, attracting the uncomplimentary nicknames 'Flying Pig' and 'Warthog'. This example was actually built after nationalisation, in 1949, and was withdrawn in 1966.

The goods shed on the right has now given way to the loading area of the local Co-op store. The Co-operative movement has a long history in the town. Local men founded the Desborough Co-operative Society in 1863, which grew to include local shops, a corset and lingerie factory (making products under the 'Desbeau' brand), a bank, a supermarket, travel agent, funeral director and local ironstone quarries. It is now part of the East Midlands Co-operative Society group. *R. C. Riley, Transport Treasury collection/WA*

DESBOROUGH was justly famous for the veteran signals at the end of the down platform, a short Midland lower-quadrant Starting signal above 'splitting Distants' for Desborough North. The rear of the signal can be seen here in this view of the station looking east on 10 June 1960.

The station platforms having disappeared, the 'present' view is taken from the adjacent road bridge. The station house survives on the right, with the Co-op store and industrial buildings on the former goods yard beyond. *H. C. Casserley/WA*

Right In the grass on the west side of the road bridge is a small post carrying a still-relevant 'Warning – Limited Clearance' enamel sign. Happily this has also meant the survival of two pairs of semaphore signal wire pulleys attached to it. *WA*

DESBOROUGH NORTH signal box stood at the summit of the line in Northamptonshire, and breasting the summit with the 1.00pm train from Leicester through to Cambridge via Kettering and Huntingdon is Ivatt 2MT 2-6-0 No 46444, on Easter Monday 22 April 1957. (This was another LMS-design loco built during the early years of nationalisation in 1949.) As viewed from what is known as 'Judges Bridge', there are up and down goods loops beside the passenger lines, and the signal box is just off the extreme right-hand edge of the picture. The down goods line extended as far as the next box at Braybrook, but the up goods, on the constant 1 in 132/133 climb from Market Harborough, extended all the way from Little Bowden Junction, just south of Market Harborough, where the line is in Leicestershire. Everything except the two running lines has gone. *Michael Mensing/WA*

PIDDINGTON: The Midland railway's branch from its new London main line at Oakley Junction, north of Bedford, via Olney to Northampton St John's Street opened in 1872; it entered the county at Ravenstone Wood Junction (see Volume 65) and the only intermediate station in Northamptonshire was at Piddington. Remotely located, it was nearer the village of Horton, whose name it carried on opening. In 1876 it became Piddington & Horton, probably to avoid confusion with Horton (-in-Ribblesdale), opened that year on the Settle & Carlisle line; in 1904 Horton was dropped. An Olney resident, the late Ivor Neale, recalled: 'It was a small station in the middle of nowhere, miles from the village that bore its name... The station was always kept very clean and tidy with colourful flowerbeds in the spring and summer. Very seldom was there more than one passenger seen to get on or off.' That atmosphere is exemplified by this photograph taken on 17 July 1959, as a four-wheel railbus approaches forming the 12.23pm departure for Bedford; the railbuses had been introduced the previous year in an attempt to halt the line's decline.

Despite that innovation Piddington station closed in March 1962, and the line in 1964, although a Ministry of Defence depot here (behind the camera) kept the Northampton end open, in MoD ownership from 1968 and singled by 1969, until it was lifted in the 1980s. The second view shows the closed station during that era, looking in the other direction in November 1973. The substantial station building still stands today in splendid isolation, and in private ownership. *John Spencer Gilks/Peter Butler*

HARDINGSTONE JUNCTION: On the approach to Northampton the Midland line crossed the LNWR Blisworth-Peterborough line, then ran parallel with it to Hardingstone Junction, where there was a connection between the two. The signal box stood between the two lines; seen here in the mid-1960s, looking west, is the 1938 LMS replacement for the original MR structure, which had been on the east side of the footpath. The former LNWR line is immediately out of the picture on the left, while the MR line continues past the box to its Far Cotton goods station on Bridge Street, across the road from the LNWR station, and a temporary station opened in 1866 for services from Wellingborough. Unseen behind the signal box, the passenger lines used to curve to the right towards the later St John's Street. The building in the distance is the former MR loco shed (1873-1924).

The signal box closed in 1970 and in 2012 only the top of the roof of that shed, now a listed building, gives a clue to the location, although I am standing on the footpath seen in the 'past' picture. The Midland metals are long gone, but fragments of the LNWR line survive in what until relatively recent times had been a permanent way depot. These will, however, eventually disappear as this large area of wasteland is due to be redeveloped. *John Spencer/WA*

This is the view looking east on 26 November 1934, as an unidentified train approaches from the Bedford line (is it a steam railmotor with trailer, or a push-pull unit with the loco invisible at the far end…?). It is signalled to go round into St John's Street, while on the adjacent ex-LNWR line a train is signalled towards Bridge Street station. In 1939, on the closure of St John's Street, this junction was completely reversed, so that trains to and from Bedford could access the ex-LNWR line direct. *Peter Butler collection*

NORTHAMPTON ST JOHN'S STREET: Having crossed the River Nene, the line passed between what is now Beckets Park and the cattle market, then crossed Victoria Promenade by this girder bridge. This photograph was taken in 1948, nearly ten years after the station had closed, and it appears that the bridge may be in course of demolition.

The embankment on the right of the picture still exists, and the bridge abutment was where the brick retaining wall stands below the trees; the bridge crossed what is now a roundabout, and the former cattle market site on the right has become a Morrisons supermarket. The older buildings on the left have been replaced by St John's multi-storey car park, although there's a fragment of old red-brick wall that may be the one seen on the extreme left of the 'past' picture. *Bill Meredith, Peter Butler collection/WA*

NORTHAMPTON ST JOHN'S STREET is seen here from the signal box in the year that it closed, 1939. It faced St John's Street on the right, and was elevated on the left-hand side as the ground sloped away. It was built on land purchased by the MR in 1871 from the former 12th-century St John's Priory, and boasted a large elegant building of a light-coloured limestone and a train shed that covered the central part of the two platforms. There was no footbridge, so passengers crossed between platforms by the barrow crossing in the foreground.

With all three of Northampton's stations coming under LMS ownership in 1923, it was clear that St John's Street (the distinguishing suffix given to it by the LMS in 1924) was the least viable, so as a cost-cutting exercise it was closed on 3 July 1939, and, as mentioned above, Hardingstone Junction was converted so that trains could use Bridge Street and Castle instead. Following closure the lines were used as sidings and for the storage of rolling stock. In 1948 the station building was converted into offices, but was finally demolished in the 1960s to make way for a car park. The nearly equivalent 'present' view is looking across that car park from the adjacent multi-storey; the row of terraced houses on the left fixes the scene. Since this picture was taken in the summer of 2012 the car park has been dug up to accommodate new buildings for the university, so the 'present' is already the 'past'! *Bill Meredith, Peter Butler collection/WA*

This is the view looking away from the platform ends on 24 March 1939, with the signal box and bridge over Victoria Promenade on the right, and the loco turntable and houses in Swan Street on the left. *Bill Meredith, Peter Butler collection*

NORTHAMPTON ST JOHN'S STREET: 'Freedom is in peril. Defend it with all your might.' The date is 1 October 1939 and Britain has been at war with Germany for four weeks. This the far end of the station, with St John's Street descending towards Bridge Street. Beyond the station was a carriage shed, and there seems to be stock in it and at the platform, even though the station has been closed since July. Blocks of flats occupy the site today.
Bill Meredith, Peter Butler collection/WA

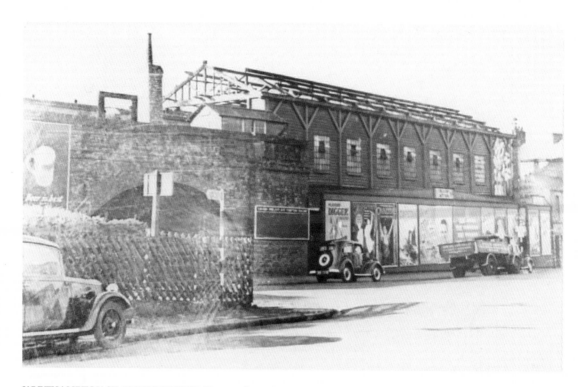

NORTHAMPTON ST JOHN'S STREET: The carriage shed is seen again, also in October 1939. The lower entrance to the station forecourt is beyond the typically Midland diagonal fencing, and a subway passes beneath the tracks to link with a footpath at the rear of Victoria Gardens on the far side. The classic posters are advertising, among other products, Player's 'Digger' and Wills's 'Capstan' cigarettes, Bovril and Ovaltine.

The location of the subway is now part of a one-way road system at the bottom of Bridge Street, which cuts through the station site to link with Victoria Gardens and Victoria Promenade beyond.

St John's Street station was originally intended to be a 'through' station, as plans had been drawn up in 1874 to extend the line across Bridge Street and westwards to Blisworth to connect with the Northampton & Banbury Junction Railway, but nothing came of the idea.*Bill Meredith, Peter Butler collection/WA*

Higham Ferrers branch

IRCHESTER JUNCTION: The 5¼-mile Higham Ferrers branch (originally intended to have gone through to Raunds) was built at the instigation of Rushden's boot and shoe manufacturers, who wanted a more convenient outlet for their products than Irchester and Irthlingborough stations. It opened on 1 May 1894, connecting with the slow/goods lines of the Midland Railway's main line at Irchester Junction, which had no signals on the passenger lines. On 19 September 1964, after regular passenger services had ceased, 'The Cobbler' rail tour collects the single-line token from the signalman before proceeding onto the branch; the loco is ex-LMS 4F 0-6-0 No 44260. The box closed just before Christmas in 1969.

The grassy cutting is all that remains of the start of the Higham branch today. When the cutting was excavated, iron ore was discovered, so this was quarried for a year before the line itself opened. As seen elsewhere, the slow line is now a single track Beyond the site of the junction is Wellingborough Viaduct over the River Nene, and in the distance the town of Wellingborough itself. It can be seen that the two sets of lines are at different levels, as the slow/goods lines rise at a gentler gradient towards the 'Wymington deviation' alongside (and beneath) Sharnbrook summit. *Peter Butler collection/WA*

NEAR IRCHESTER JUNCTION: Once round the corner from the junction, the line crossed the broad valley of a small tributary of the River Nene. Running tender-first with the empty stock to form the Saturdays-only through train to Leicester on 6 August 1956 is ex-LMS 4P 4-4-0 No 41095, which ended its life at Gloucester Barnwood shed two years later.

The line here is still readily recognisable and open as a farmland access road. This is the view towards the bridge over the stream, and the overbridge near Irchester Junction. Between the latter bridge and the former junction, the aforementioned cutting is now filled to the brim with an evil-smelling 'slurry lagoon'! *Robin Cullup collection/WA*

RUSHDEN: Before arriving at Rushden station the line crossed the High Street (formerly the A6) by a girder bridge, which offered a clearance of only 14ft 3in. It is seen first on 11 January 1970, less than a year after goods traffic finally ceased. Note the man perched precariously at the top of the telegraph pole on the extreme right!

Three years later the bridge is being removed. The posters on the railway embankment show that in the intervening years decimalisation has arrived, and a cheap day return to London (from Wellingborough, presumably) has gone up from 24 shillings (£1.20) to £1.85.

Today the bridge no longer presents an obstruction to tall vehicles. The former Queen Victoria Hotel beyond the bridge, with its distinctive Victorian roof architecture, is now divided into flats, and an Asda supermarket has appeared opposite. *Peter Butler (2)/ WA*

RUSHDEN station looks neat and tidy on 13 April 1959, two months before closure. The view is looking towards Higham Ferrers, and it can be seen that the site was laid out for double track, as originally envisaged by the authorising Act, but it was only ever a single line.

The second view is during the 'wilderness years' between closure and rescue. It is July 1972 and all seems intact bar the track, while foliage gradually takes over. The young boy in the foreground is the photographer's son, now a Train Manager for First Great Western!

Following closure in 1959 the station site and buildings were bought by Northamptonshire County Council in 1976/77 and rented to various businesses, the council itself using the goods shed as a depot. Then in 1984 the Rushden Historical Transport Society, founded in 1976, obtained a lease on the building. The RHTS Social Club established a famed real ale bar in 1985, and a museum opened the following year. In 1990 the site was threatened by a new road development, for which purpose NCC had purchased it in the first place, but this was averted and finally, in 1996, the RHTS was able to acquire the freehold. By 2012 the foliage is under control in the form of platform flower beds, while visitors enjoy refreshments on the platform, and parked carriages offer various attractions within. The footbridge has had to be dismantled, but the footpath is maintained across the site; hopefully a bridge will be reinstated at some time in the future. *R. M. Casserley/Peter Butler/WA*

RUSHDEN station was initially considered rather indifferent in terms of its accommodation, so the Midland extended it between 1905 and 1910. The street side of the single-storey building on the rising site is seen here in 1984; note the Midland-pattern diagonal fencing.

The restored building, complete with enamel advertising signs, is seen in 2012, accompanied by a new generation of road sign! In the background can be glimpsed the station signal box, formerly at East Langton on the Midland main line between Market Harborough and Wigston, which arrived at Rushden in 1986. *N. D. Mundy, Peter Butler collection/WA*

RUSHDEN: With only a fortnight of passenger services left, BR Standard 2MT 2-6-2T No 84006 propels the 4.10pm service from Higham towards Wellingborough, pausing at Rushden on 28 May 1959. In 1954 the steam push-pull train had been replaced by a new diesel multiple unit, but the experiment didn't last.

In April 1959 it was confirmed that the branch was to close with effect from Saturday 13 June. On that day we see one of the last trains calling at Rushden. There are still a few passengers, and a healthy-looking heap of parcels on the trolley beyond the porter.

The line was only 65 years old when it closed, but 53 years *after* closure it continues to thrive as a railway heritage centre! Today there's plenty to enjoy here, with occasional steam train rides on the three-quarters of a mile of track laid towards Higham Ferrers. *Peter Butler collection/Les Hanson/WA*

RUSHDEN: The branch opened for goods traffic on 1 September 1893, nine months before passenger services started. Rushden station boasted a large goods shed, seen in the distance of this 4 September 1969 photograph, taken from the bridge carrying a footpath to Shirley Road; the shed was doubled in length in the early years of the 20th century. Despite the fact that the line is on the brink of closure, ten years after the cessation of regular passenger trains, there is a substantial number of mineral wagons in the yard, and considerable stocks of coal; even within a few days of closure goods trains of up to 20 wagons were still arriving. It is recorded that in 1947 the goods depot employed 11 clerks and 32 other workmen, with six mechanical drays and six horse-drawn ones.

Coal traffic and iron sand from Ferrersands gravel pits at Higham kept the branch alive until 1 November 1969. Within a year the track had been lifted, but, as mentioned above, the station and goods yard sites passed into County Council ownership. By 1996 the station was safely in the hands of the Rushden Historical Transport Society, and this 1999 photograph shows the trackbed east of Rushden being prepared to receive track once more. The goods shed is still being used by the council.

In 2005 a new road cut through the site, separating station and goods shed. It was named John Clark Way after a prominent local shoe manufacturer, businessman and landowner who had died in 1924. In the 2012 picture a new access road is being cut into the embankment on the extreme left-hand side of the picture for the enlarged Denfield Park Primary School; it was subsequently named Bob Whitworth Way, after a former headmaster. Rails now once again pass beneath the footbridge. *Peter Butler (2)/WA*

RUSHDEN: The previously mentioned footbridge can be seen in the background of this view looking back towards Rushden station. On the right is the ground frame that operated the points for what is described in Midland Railway plans as 'Rushden & Higham Ferrers District Gas Works Siding'. The gas works had opened in 1892, and coal was delivered here until 1968, when the advent of North Sea gas made the works redundant. In this view, taken at about that time, the siding is being lifted.

The bridge has been recently repaired but is not safe to use. However, track has been relaid here, and alongside it is the new 2010 Greenway foot and cycle path linking Rushden and Higham Ferrers; with funding from Sustrans and the Department of Transport through the Links to Schools programme, the intention of such routes is to connect schools and their communities to the National Cycle Network. The Greenway also provides an ideal viewing point for when steam trains are running! The kink in the fence in the centre of the picture is where the siding ran, and the buffer stops are on the site of the ground frame – the house chimney above them is the same as the one seen above the ground frame in the 'past' view. *Peter Butler collection/WA*

RUSHDEN: To prove that today's 'present' is tomorrow's 'past', this view was taken looking the other way in the summer of 2004. The former railway trackbed is on the extreme left, and John Clark Way is being constructed on the right. In the middle is an old quarry, opposite the gas works siding, which was also rail-connected.

In 2012 the scene is quite different. The railway and Greenway are seen on the left, and an industrial estate has appeared on the horizon, adjacent to the new A6 Rushden and Higham bypass. Extensive housing development at 'Church View' is spreading on the right. *Peter Butler/WA*

HIGHAM FERRERS station was located in a broad area of land behind the town off the inevitably-named Midland Road. It consisted of a single platform with a run-round loop and a siding at the Rushden end, where the station's ground frame was located; this can just be glimpsed by the bridge on the site of the present-day Queensway, which now links the town with the Ferrers Specialist Arts College built later on land to the left of the railway. In LMS days, on 10 August 1945, 1P 0-4-4T No 1246 is preparing to propel the 4.15pm push-pull train back to Wellingborough; the driver is leaning from his cab at the front of the train, while the fireman will stay on the footplate to attend to the locomotive. This 1875 veteran would have become No 58031 on nationalisation, but was scrapped in 1949 before the number could be applied.

The second view is dated 18 May 1959, a few weeks short of closure, and we can see the driver's end of the labelled 'pull & push' train. There's not much activity on this spring day.

Beyond the station's run-round loop were two sidings, one of which passed through the stone-build goods shed. In the foreground of the third picture is the ground frame to operate the points, as ex-MR 4F 0-6-0 No 43861 (1918-63) shunts a modest goods train on 29 June 1955.

After the end of passenger services in 1959 goods and postal trains continued to serve the station for another ten years, and even the occasional special or holiday excursion was seen until 1968. Since then all the buildings have been demolished, and the site has been subsumed by a heavily fortified industrial estate, so a present-day equivalent picture is impossible. The 2012 view is looking towards the station from the site of the bridge in the background of the 1945 photograph, where Queensway now crosses the Greenway from Rushden, which terminates here.
H. C. Casserley/Frank Hornby/H. C. Casserley/WA

Kettering-Harringworth

CORBY: The Midland's new line from Manton Junction, on the Leicester-Peterborough line, to Glendon South Junction, north of Kettering, provided the MR with a second set of tracks south towards London. Involving heavy engineering, it opened in 1879 for goods traffic and 1880 for passenger trains. The first station north of Kettering was at Geddington, which closed as early as 1948, then came Corby & Cottingham, as it was originally known. Not long after opening it was renamed Weldon, then Weldon & Corby. In 1937 the LMS reversed the name, then in 1957 BR dropped the '& Weldon'. Corby station closed on 18 April 1966, leaving this sizeable steel town as one of the largest in the UK without a passenger rail service! However, after much campaigning the station re-opened on 13 April 1987, with financial support from Corby Council, to accommodate an experimental shuttle service from Kettering. On 25 April the recently re-opened station is busy with passengers as a Class 108 DMU loads up ready to return to Kettering.

The experiment lasted until 4 June 1990, when funding was withdrawn, the station closed once more, and a dedicated shuttle bus took over. Following privatisation, in 2006 the Department of Transport insisted that renewal of the Midland main line franchise must include provision of a station at Corby. East Midlands Trains won the franchise, and the new station opened in 2009. This view from the new station shows the former down platform, which had been used by the shuttle trains.
Frank Hornby/WA

CORBY: This broader view, looking north on an unknown date, but after '& Weldon' had been dropped from the name in 1957, shows both platforms, the footbridge and the station building as a mineral train disappears beneath Cottingham Road bridge towards the steelworks site. It corresponds approximately with the 'past' view opposite.

After the short-lived reopening in 1987-90, the site was once more abandoned. In 2007 Network Rail announced that it had allocated £1.2 million for the new station, and the 15 April 2008 photograph, (*right*) looking south from Cottingham Road bridge, shows site clearance work under way.

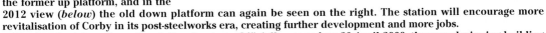

The new station is on the site of the former up platform, and in the 2012 view (*below*) the old down platform can again be seen on the right. The station will encourage more revitalisation of Corby in its post-steelworks era, creating further development and more jobs.

The fourth picture shows the station frontage. Officially opened on 30 April 2009, the award-winning building garnered both praise and criticism. *Douglas Thompson/Peter Butler/WA*

CORBY: It was during the building of railways in the county that rich seams of iron ore were exposed, providing the railway with much future traffic. An ironworks had been established in Corby by 1910, and by 1931 the population of what was then still a village was about 1,500. In 1934-35 Stewarts & Lloyds built an integrated iron and steel plant and the population burgeoned, reaching 12,000 by 1939. Corby was declared a New Town in 1950 and boom-time expansion continued. In 1967 the steel industry was nationalised, and the Corby works became

part of the British Steel Corporation. However, in 1973 the Government decided to concentrate steel-making at coastal locations with easy access to imported ore, and from 1975 steel-making at Corby was phased out – closure was announced in 1979, and some 11,000 jobs were lost. Tube-making continued, and in the intervening years considerable national and local enterprise and investment has seen the town rise phoenix-like from the ashes of its potentially catastrophic industrial demise.

These views were taken from Cottingham Road bridge looking north towards the works. In the first, dated 1 June 1958, ex-LMS 'Jubilee' 4-6-0 No 45590 *Travancore* (a former kingdom of southern India) heads towards Corby station with a Nottingham-St Pancras express. The two lines on the right are shunting necks from the works.

Seen from the other side of the line, on 6 July 1961 'Peak' Type 4 No D33, new into traffic the previous month, heads south beneath Rockingham Road bridge with the up 'Waverley' Edinburgh-St Pancras express. Tucked in beside the road bridge in both pictures is Lloyds Sidings South signal box.

The third, broader view is dated 20 July 1974, in the last years of the steelworks.

Today, as so often in this book, the former open aspect of the industrial-era railway has been reduced to a narrow wooded corridor. The single line north from Corby station here divides to form four tracks once more, those on the right being sidings, but the line northwards now carries mainly freight, a couple of regular passenger services and the occasional special or diverted passenger train. *R. C. Riley, Transport Treasury collection/ Robin Cullup collection/Peter Butler/ WA*

CORBY STEELWORKS: These pictures were all taken from Rockingham Road bridge, looking north towards the fan of sidings on the up side of the line serving the steelworks and controlled by Lloyds Sidings South signal box. The first undated but LMS-era photograph shows ex-MR 3F 0-6-0 No 3832 passing (or arriving at?) the works with a southbound mineral train. It looks as though the rake of five wagons on the right behind the steam from the loco's safety valve is being loose shunted into the sidings by the loco on the extreme right of the picture.

The second view is a commercial postcard of 'The Works'. In the right background can be seen the exhaust from two of the steelworks' saddle tanks.

On Monday 19 June 1961 the Queen and the Duke of Edinburgh visited Corby by train, to visit various developments in the New Town and have lunch at Stewarts & Lloyds' steelworks. The third photograph shows the Royal Train passing on the down fast line, having deposited the Royal visitors at the station, with a good number of interested works employees watching from the sidings.

We move forward to 20 July 1974 for the fourth view, with an internal diesel shunter and two tipper wagons right of centre, and some track panels indicating rationalisation of the sidings. In something over five years all this would be gone.

Today the steelworks site is occupied by the aptly named Phoenix Centre of retail and industrial units. The sidings on the right look little-used today.
Transport Treasury collection/Robin Cullup collection (2)/Peter Butler/ WA

GRETTON: After Corby the line begins a long descent at 1 in 200 through Corby Tunnel (1,926 yards) to emerge on the south side of the valley of the River Welland. The next station is Gretton, on a high embankment. The 'past' view is looking south-west up the gradient towards Corby; it is undated, but may be after closure on 18 April 1966, as there is no sign of life and a general unkempt air.

All traces of the platforms have since disappeared. The 'present' view is taken from the top of the access steps from road level, cleverly built into the viaduct over Station Road, the first arch of which also provided a subway between the platforms. Note the attractive iron railing on the viaduct. *Douglas Thompson/WA*

Opposite The main picture shows the access stairs built into the sides of the viaduct. Between the last big arch and the end of the viaduct is a smaller 'tunnel' through the bridge forming a subway between the platforms.

The inset view shows the matching steps on the up (north) side of the viaduct, and the station building at the Manton end of the up platform, which survives as a private house.

Two miles beyond Gretton was Harringworth station, which, like Geddington, closed on 1 November 1948, then follows the famous Harringworth Viaduct (see page 6), which carries the line across the Welland and into Rutland. *Both WA*

Kettering-Huntingdon

NEAR BARTON SEAGRAVE: Our final railway journey in Northamptonshire takes us along the Midland Railway's bucolic Kettering-Huntingdon branch, which connected with the GN/GE Joint line and GER line through St Ives to Cambridge. Promoted by the Kettering, Thrapstone (sic) & Huntingdon Railway, it opened to passenger traffic on 1 March 1866 and was worked from the outset by the MR, which absorbed it in 1897. Leaving the Midland main line at Pytchley Junction (see page 67), the line climbed steeply at 1 in 70. Climbing that bank and passing milepost 1 with the 2.10pm Kettering-Cambridge train on 18 May 1959 is Ivatt 2MT 2-6-0 No 46403.

The line closed to passenger trains shortly afterwards, on Saturday 13 June (officially from Monday 15th, but there were no Sunday trains), although this end of the line remained open for goods and mineral traffic until 1978. Presumably not enough people wanted to travel between Kettering and Cambridge, but ironically in the

early 1990s the 'A1-M1 Link Road' – the A14 – passed Kettering on its way to the M11 at Cambridge, and for some miles occupies the route of the old MR branch, as here at Polwell Lane, Barton Seagrave. The railway would have run somewhere among the trees on the right; to give an idea of the gradient, the A14 crosses the Midland main line in the dip in the distance. *Ken Fairey/ WA*

NEAR BARTON SEAGRAVE: Looking the other way from Polwell Lane bridge, we witness the unusual sight of an ex-LMS 'Jubilee' express passenger 4-6-0 on the branch: No 45660 *Rooke* is on an iron-ore train from Twywell on 12 May 1965. The loco was withdrawn and scrapped just over a year later.

The delightful rural tranquillity of the line here has since been rudely shattered by the 24/7 roar of the A14, constructed around 1990 and seen here unusually quiet on 14 June 2012. A lorry belonging to Antwerp-based Cobelfret approaches; this major international shipping company was formed in 1928, six years before *Rooke* was built, and demonstrates that 25% of freight traffic on the A14 is international. *Ken Fairey/WA*

Left BUTLIN'S SIDINGS: *Rooke* is seen again on the same day during its sojourn on the line, running towards Twywell tender-first with the iron-ore 'trip' working. The empty wagons belong to the Lancashire Steel Manufacturing Co Ltd of Irlam near Manchester. The location is Butlin's Sidings, near Cranford, where there was a signal box of that name controlling access to several ironstone quarries operated by Butlin, Bevan & Co. The photograph was taken from 'Black Bridge', which carried a minor road from the old A604 Kettering-Huntingdon road to Burton Latimer – the 'Major Road Ahead' sign at the junction can be seen on the left above the second wagon.

When the A14 was built the minor road was closed, but the route was eventually reinstated by the construction of a footbridge across the dual carriageway. In this 2012 view from that bridge, a police car is passing the former road junction on the left, and the same electricity cable route can be seen on the horizon. *Ken Fairey/WA*

Below CRANFORD station was, unusually for this line, right in the village it served. The attractive stone station buildings are seen here probably in the mid-1960s. There used to be a small Midland Railway signal box, effectively a covered ground frame, at the far end of the platform, but that has gone by this time, although there is still a goods loop and siding accommodation.

The station closed to passengers on 2 April 1956, but goods traffic lingered on until 6 November 1961. The building has since been converted into an elegant private house and is now inaccessible and invisible from this angle. *John Spencer/WA*

CRANFORD QUARRY: There were rail-connected quarries east and west of Cranford station, but those to the east were the most extensive, with workings both north and south of the line. These eventually became the largest open-cast workings in the area, and there were exchange sidings at Cranford East capable of accommodating 143 ore wagons. In the first view an unidentified 0-6-0 saddle tank has emerged from the bridge beneath the A604 Kettering-Huntingdon road, heading for the 'main line'.

In the second picture we are now looking from that bridge towards the quarry's sheds and sidings on a snowy day in the winter of 1969. The Huntingdon branch crosses the scene in the distance; on the left, beyond the tree, can be glimpsed some wagons in the exchange sidings.

The bridge under the road has been filled in, but in another 'Tony Robinson moment' I discovered the shallow cutting that had contained the sheds, and scrambled down into it; however, it is now effectively a small overgrown wood and photography was pointless. The A14 now severs the scene between the sheds and the Huntingdon branch. *Robin Cullup collection/Peter Butler*

TWYWELL station was a couple of miles further on. Although only a modest station with no passing loop, it was provided with a full-size Midland-pattern signal box in 1906 as iron-ore quarrying in the district increased and new sidings were laid. The box and the down Starting signal can be seen in this undated view, although the station still seems to be in use; it closed on 30 July 1951, and the signal box remained in use until 1953. Goods traffic, however, survived to the end; at the far end of the platform a loading dock was later constructed where iron ore could be tipped from lorries into wagons. The last commercial traffic was iron concentrate, loaded at Higham Ferrers until 1969, and the last train ran officially on 20 January 1978; the very last train was a diesel-hauled brake-van special, the 'Twywell Flyer', on 18 March of that year.

Today the station house is a private dwelling and its extensive gardens cover the platform area and trackbed. These photographs were taken from the A604 bridge, but the A14 severed this road between the station and Twywell village, and this stretch is now effectively no more than a drive to a house in the valley by the road. The white lines and 'catseyes' are still there but, like the road near Towcester station illustrated in Volume 65, this is a picture of a disused railway taken from a disused road! *Douglas Thompson/ WA*

TWYWELL: Half a mile beyond the station, as the line descended towards the Nene valley, it crossed a minor road between Woodford and Twywell, where there was also (and still is) a ford through one of the Nene's tributaries. This undated LMS-era photograph shows a Fowler 7F 0-8-0 (possibly one of Kettering's allocation) taking empty wagons back to Kettering from Islip Furnaces. Apparently during the war Americans based at nearby Grafton Underwood airfield used the ford to wash their lorries; there were, of course, washing facilities at the airbase, but not half a dozen pubs, which were to be found in Woodford at that time!

The A14 has obliterated the trackbed at this point, and speeding across the rather larger and more substantial bridge in 2012 are two articulated lorries. The leading one carries a P&O NedLloyd container. P&O (Peninsular & Oriental Shipping Company) is as old as railways, having been founded in 1837, while the ancestor of NedLloyd, Netherland Line (NED for short), was founded in Amsterdam in 1870. They merged in 1997 in a $4.7 billion acquisition, and the company is now part of the giant Danish shipping line Maersk, whose first ship sailed in 1928, a year or so before the Fowler 0-8-0 was built. Such global enterprises make the original scope of the Kettering-Cambridge line seem very parochial! *Robin Cullup collection/WA*

THRAPSTON MIDLAND ROAD: Just east of that bridge the line passed, and served, Islip Furnaces; these were supplied from quarries that boasted the largest narrow-gauge railway system anywhere in the ironstone industry – 10 miles of 3-foot-gauge track – which remained in operation until 1952. Also serving the ironworks was the LNWR's Nene Valley line, via a spur almost a mile long from sidings adjacent to where the MR crossed the LNWR line at right-angles (see page 31). The Huntingdon line then climbed to gain the eastern side of the Nene Valley, crossing the river by a handsome nine-arch brick viaduct (replacing an earlier metal structure) and entering the sharply curved Thrapston Midland Road station ('Midland Road' being a 1924 LMS addition to distinguish it from Bridge Street – the two stations, once rivals, were now bedfellows). At some time in the 1950s an ex-GER 'J15' 0-6-0 enters the station with a Cambridge-bound service; at this time a Cambridge loco worked the first westbound train of the day, and returned with the last train from Kettering.

Apart from the track having been lifted, the station survived almost intact for many years following closure to passengers on 15 June 1959 and goods (Kettering-Kimbolton) on 28 October 1963, then the south-east end of the site was severed when the A14 was built in the late 1980s. At that time the signal box (minus its frame) and, I believe, the waiting shelter seen here were acquired by Sir William McAlpine for his private Fawley Hill Railway in Buckinghamshire. Then sadly the station building and goods shed were burned down by arsonists, and this is the site today – the line of bricks just left of centre is the edge of the Kettering-bound platform. The station site and a small quarry area behind it are currently earmarked for housing development, so soon all trace of the station will be lost. *Douglas Thompson/WA*

THRAPSTON MIDLAND ROAD:
This is the view looking towards
Raunds and Huntingdon. Thrapston
was the first station out from
Kettering to have a passenger train
passing loop. Note that the
platforms were staggered, so that
the barrow crossing at the end of
the left-hand (up) platform
connected with the middle of the
down platform, so there had to be
a dip to accommodate it. There
were water cranes at the end of
both platforms, fed from the water
tower glimpsed in the previous
'past' photograph.

The second view dates from the
second half of the 1980s, and the
station was then still in almost
complete condition as offices, the
most obvious addition being the
building spanning the trackbed.

Thus it remained until destroyed
by fire and demolished. A pile of
debris marks the location today,
awaiting the housing development.
A lorry crosses the far end of the
site on the A14. *LGRP/WA (2)*

BEYOND THRAPSTON trains faced a 2-mile climb out of the valley at 1 in 80, and tackling the gradient in fine style with a Cambridge train is Ivatt 2MT 2-6-0 No 46495. I have a particular fondness for this photograph, for several reasons. The location is just a few hundred yards from where I now live, and No 46495 entered traffic in 1952, the same year that I 'arrived'. It was allocated new to Kettering to work the Cambridge line, then by the mid-1960s it was resident shunter in Coventry yard, adjacent to my school; on summer afternoons when the windows were open my trainspotting friends and I could here 46495 going about its business, and wished we could be at the lineside watching! Upon withdrawal in October 1966 the 2-6-0 'came home' to Kettering to be cut up at Cohen's yard on the outskirts of the town the following year.

An overbridge close to this spot partially collapsed during the harsh winter of 1962/63, which prompted closure of this part of the line. Following the passage of the final goods train in October 1963 the line was lifted, and the cutting was taken over by nature. In the spring of 1995 the farmer cleared it and laid the hedges, and I grabbed the opportunity to take a 'present' equivalent of Mr Groom's picture, just in case I should ever do a 'Past and Present' book... The remains of the platelayers' hut on the extreme left are still to be found, but today the cutting is once more abandoned to nature, muntjac deer, foxes and rabbits. *P. H. Groom/WA*

RAUNDS station was some 2 miles from the centre of the town it purported to serve, on top of the hills at the extreme east of the county, and was thus poorly patronised. The 12-lever signal box on the extreme left of the photograph, a replacement opened in 1891, was normally switched out, as here on Friday 18 July 1958; it was only opened when access to the goods yard was required. Although it was a block post, single-line tokens were not exchanged here.

Like Thrapston, the station closed to passenger traffic less than a year later, in June 1959, and the same view looking south-east from the Raunds-Keyston road is now impossible due to trees growing on the trackbed in what is now the sizeable garden of the refurbished and extended station house. The house is seen from the former station entrance, now providing access to the premises of Auto Spares & Salvage Ltd, which occupies the goods yard today. *R. M. Casserley/WA*

RAUNDS: At about 5.50pm on the same day the Casserleys photographed ex-GER No 65457, a veteran 1906 'J15' 0-6-0, leaving Raunds with the 5.25pm Kettering-Cambridge train. Friday was market day in Kettering, and two occupied cattle wagons head the train. The goods shed is on the right; the yard sidings had a capacity for 66 wagons, but there appears to be just one van in the shed.

By kind permission of the current occupiers, I was able to capture a similar view more than half a century later. The site is now a busy and sophisticated car spares and salvage operation, but the goods shed is still in use, and some drain covers cast with the initials 'MR' can also be seen. During my visit one of the site staff told me that his great-grandfather had helped draw up the plans for the station. Talking of scrap, No 65457 was withdrawn from Cambridge shed in 1962.

Thus our journey across Northamptonshire ends in this remote and peaceful spot, where the line traverses the undulating landscape towards Kimbolton and Cambridge, leaving the county just over 2 miles east of Raunds. And I have just a short journey home. *H. C. Casserley/WA*

INDEX OF LOCATIONS